THE OTHER SIDE OF BURNOUT:
SOLUTIONS FOR HEALTHCARE PROFESSIONALS

Melissa Wolf, MD

Shaun J. Gillis, MD

First published by Dog Ear Publishing
4011 Vincennes Rd
Indianapolis, IN 46268
www.dogearpublishing.net

ISBN: 978-1-4575-5700-2

This book is printed on acid-free paper.

Printed in the United States of America

CONTENTS

DEDICATION

For physicians

PREFACE

Although some of our text may seem edgy, we have absolutely written this book with genuine love and respect for the clinical practice of medicine, in heartfelt compassion for our colleagues, and with every desire to present tangible relief from the epidemic of physician burnout. We have intentionally written the uncensored (and sometimes painfully raw) truth about our experiences and what we feel are both pervasive problems and workable solutions for professionals in crisis. At times, we have knowingly shared stories about ourselves that expose our flaws and shortcomings, as well as the strategies we have used to overcome them as we continue to navigate the complexities of life and medicine.

We have also specifically written in an informal analytical and anecdotal format, with full knowledge of and appreciation for the comprehensive body of published data available on the topic of burnout. We have intentionally described our ideas in a nonscientific manner so as to connect intimately with readers and to acknowledge that though research study results hold inherent value, they often don't specifically describe the experiences of individual people. We hope that with our more informal approach, individual doctors may more readily recognize components of their own plight and be inspired to take meaningful action accordingly.

Likewise, we recognize the clear and persuasive benefits of mindfulness practice in the workplace, which much has been written about. We love the idea of mindfulness and suggest it liberally; however, as one of our colleagues most eloquently stated, "You can't readily meditate your way out of an overbooked schedule." Our chapters, therefore, attempt to directly tackle some of the tangible hassles facing providers, without detracting from the existing body of useful data already in print. We hope to do more than simply characterize the nature of burnout and instead, encourage solutions-focused thinking for individuals and organizations.

Lastly, the ideas presented here were formed in collaborative effort over a year's worth of Monday-afternoon brainstorming "tea times" in coffee shops around town. Although our personalities and backgrounds are different, we discovered a shared passion for understanding physician burnout and trialing solutions. Although I, Melissa, happen to be the one typing and scribing our thoughts onto these pages, the concepts are in no way solely mine. This book represents the best of our joint attempt at conveying our experiences and observations on burnout to colleagues in crisis and at proposing practical solutions that both individuals and institutions can immediately implement for relief. We sincerely hope that our stories resonate and that our ideas help revive enthusiasm for the clinical practice of medicine.

Shaun J. Gillis, MD
Melissa Wolf, MD

A NOTE TO NONPHYSICIAN READERS

We have written this book for physicians because we are physicians and feel specifically qualified to describe our experience and expertise as clinicians in the field of medicine. That being said, we wholeheartedly acknowledge that nurses, physician assistants, nurse practitioners, midwives, sonographers, and all other healthcare professionals entrenched in our modern system have firsthand experience with burnout. While we can't know or comprehend the details of your specific perspectives, we believe that many of the concepts discussed in this book may resonate with you and trigger ideas that may improve the quality of your professional lives.

In fact, even if you are not a clinician and have a career in accounting, finance, business, architecture, teaching, engineering, or any other profession, we feel the concepts in these chapters will speak to you. Our burnout examples and proposed solutions are from medicine because we are entrenched in medicine, but the ideas can be extrapolated to any person in any field who is willing to apply him- or herself creatively.

We were inspired to write after noting the suffering in ourselves and our colleagues; however, we hold special compassion for our nonphysician readers who are looking for the same burnout relief and workplace joy we find so elusive. Many thanks to those of you who are bold enough to search these pages for solutions to your own predicament. We know you will find something useful here.

A SPECIAL NOTE TO HEALTHCARE ORGANIZATIONS

Much of the burnout research and literature specifically notes the benefits of collaboration between individuals and organizations. Although we absolutely believe it is every physician's responsibility to find his or her unique path to joy, we also know this path can be more readily identified when hospitals and healthcare companies work in tandem with practitioners. To prioritize physician well-being is not to cater to the whims of an elitist or entitled few but rather to create a workplace culture founded in human decency. The extent that we feel cared for and inherently valued by our organizations, is the extent to which providers are most readily willing and able to meet the business-related goals of the companies that employ us. Our engagement stems not from sugarcoated requirements or dollars thrown in our bank accounts, but from genuine collaboration, shared objectives, and recognition of both our contributions and the limitations of our humanness. As you are likely well aware, the clinical practice of medicine is not the same as the production of widgets, and there is a level of human interaction in caregiving that cannot be additionally compressed to yield perpetually increasing appointments or corporate revenue.

To prioritize physician well-being is not to cater to the whims of an elitist or entitled few but rather to create a workplace culture founded in human decency.

In an attempt to be solutions-focused, we have added a section at the end of most chapters with suggestions for organizations to increase physician engagement. In using the term "physician engagement," we mean *true mutual collaboration*. The concept of engagement in healthcare has come to feel like a secret code that, while publicly implying mutual collaboration, behind closed doors actually means "how can we get physicians and other employees to do what we want them to do?" Our intentions in adding suggestions for organizations at the end of each chapter is to demonstrate what true physician-administration engagement might entail, and to encourage companies to support providers in achieving their highest levels of personal and professional development, not simply their highest levels of productivity or compliance.

Organizations should use caution, however. Before implementing any changes, please take our suggestions directly to your clinicians and solicit their input. What we propose may be absolutely irrelevant to the healthcare professionals in your organization, and they will no doubt have suggestions that they find more appealing. Simply asking whether your providers are experiencing burnout and how you can genuinely collaborate with them to alleviate burnout is a progressive and compassionate act.

As organizations support providers in their personal and professional development, in reviving their passion for medicine, and in their ability to work more joyfully within the parameters of the modern healthcare system, those organizations will see less physician turnover, improved patient satisfaction, fewer medical errors, greater revenue, and overall improvement in workplace morale. We appreciate your boldness in reading this text and in taking our suggestions to heart. We know you will find something useful here.

HOW TO USE THIS BOOK

We would love to simply provide every doctor and healthcare organization with a clear ten-step list to eliminate physician burnout and revive workplace engagement; however, that task is seemingly impossible. We can offer suggestions and guidance, but the landscape of modern healthcare changes constantly, and each institution has its own history and culture. Likewise, each physician has his or her own story related to medical practice. What triggers one provider may go unnoticed by another, and a solution that speaks to one practitioner may be absolutely irrelevant to a colleague.

We therefore suggest that you read through the book completely, making note of the chapters that hold the most individual relevance or trigger the most emotion for you. Then, to avoid the pitfall of overwhelm or of paralysis by analysis, go back and focus on the one, two, or three chapters that speak to you most strongly. To gain traction, start with one of our suggestions for that chapter or with your own ideas. Once you have some momentum, take the subsequent steps—one at a time—that seem most applicable to your situation.

If you feel too overwhelmed to do anything, consider reaching out to a coach, mentor, or consultant for motivation—and above all, be kind to yourself. Our personal progress in alleviating burnout has moved slowly over months and years, sometimes jumping quickly ahead and at other times feeling static or even like we are backtracking, and we certainly do not have this all figured out. Even years down the path, we still have meltdowns and moments of desperation. In staying the course, however, we've seen forward progress; overall, we simply feel better about the lives and professions we have chosen for ourselves than we did in the not-so-distant past. We know the same is possible for you once you overcome the inertia required to get started.

INTRODUCTION

Physician burnout. Fifteen years ago, these words were rarely mentioned together. Recently, however, they have become a painfully common phrase. Is it possible that physicians have become much less resilient in such a short time, or is the cause some other problem entirely? Is it honestly burnout, or have we simply lost sight of our paths in search of the lives we envisioned? Most of us were clearly resilient enough and passionate enough to earn undergraduate degrees, pass MCATs, compete for acceptance to medical school, and navigate the rigors of clerkships and residency. Many of us even accomplished these tasks while raising children, earning secondary degrees, or traveling the world. How, then, is it possible that such a hearty group is now burning out, losing passion, feeling disheartened, and questioning whether to continue contributing to society through medicine? Is our day-to-day existence so challenging that we can no longer cope, or are we frustrated doing tasks we find meaningless, with the medicine we trained for nowhere in sight?

Unfortunately, the burnout condition has reached epidemic proportions and is creating the opposite of the compassionate care we signed up to provide. Burnout leads to medical errors, substance abuse, decreased dependability, early retirement, suicide, lawsuits, and, worst of all, broken relationships. To address this disaster, we must get in tune with our true intentions, move more deliberately through our lives, and take honest inventory of our individual circumstance and careers. Instead of dwindling on the sidelines while waiting for systems to change, we must focus the lens of responsibility on ourselves. Only then will we have the power and tenacity to triumph.

By definition, burnout is not a disease but a triad of symptoms that include emotional and physical exhaustion, depersonalization and cynicism, and a diminished sense of personal accomplishment. According to surveys, more than 50 percent of physicians experience at least one of these symptoms every day; however, this doesn't entirely capture what many providers are feeling. We think the reasons behind burnout are more about a loss of ourselves and the widening gap between what we expected from the practice of medicine and what we are actually doing.

We think the reasons behind burnout are more about a loss of ourselves and the widening gap between what we expected from the practice of medicine and what we are actually doing.

The causes of burnout are many and varied but notably include increasing certification requirements, diminished autonomy, increased productivity expectations, declining career fulfillment, inefficient use of time, challenges with work-life balance, employment, electronic medical records (EMR), bureaucracy, and paperwork. For the EMR alone, it's been reported that nearly two additional hours are required for documentation and desk work for every hour of direct face time with patients. We've come to a point where physicians spend only about a third of our time seeing patients, with the remainder spent on nonclinical tasks. One physician surveyed noted that it took thirty-two clicks to order and record a flu vaccination. Additionally, many federal regulations either state explicitly or imply that the physician is the one who must do the keyboarding into the record.

The further physicians are removed from what we are passionate about, namely patient care, the more dissatisfied we become with our work. When we continue to do something unsatisfying, our excitement about medicine and our ability to care compassionately for others are slowly destroyed. The misery and regret that accompany this destruction can feed a downward spiral of isolation, depression, and suicide.

And suicide, friends, is unfortunately real. Although it's estimated that roughly 400 of our colleagues end their own lives each year, this number is likely underreported, as some deaths may not be recognized as intentional. This shocking statistic means that physicians commit suicide at an estimated rate of 28–40 per 100,000, compared to the general population rate of 12 per 100,000. Male physicians commit suicide at a rate 70 percent higher than other male professionals, and female physicians commit suicide at a rate 250–400 percent higher than that of other female professionals. More than a million patients lose their physician to suicide each year. Let that sink in for a moment.

Though we can't generalize why doctors are ending their lives despite what seems to be a fairytale career to outsiders, we believe that hopelessness sets in, at least for some providers, in part due to learned helplessness. Let's face it: We don't have much control over clinical practice anymore. We can't just take care of people and jot a note without being told what to prescribe, what to type in the chart, how many boxes to click, what meetings to attend, or how we will be reprimanded if our documentation isn't suitable for billing. In this environment, we feel reduced to shadows of what we imagined we would be in our careers, and it wreaks havoc on the core of our being.

Ultimately, we need to take time to listen to and encourage our colleagues to speak genuinely. Instead of just scrambling through our days in survival mode, we can reclaim our profession as healers. We can start with ourselves, then expand. Collectively, we are all together in this disaster, this endeavor of healthcare that has become crazier and more impossible with each passing year, and it's our challenge now, whether we envisioned modern disillusionment as part of our medical careers or not. Inherently, care of the patient requires care of the provider, and though discussions and articles abound, no one is coming to save us.

3

Inherently, care of the patient requires care of the provider, and though discussions and articles abound, no one is coming to save us.

Much has been written on this topic, and many a committee has been formed highlighting the importance of this issue, yet the problem persists. Our state medical association has a Physician Leadership Program, which repeats annually. During the excellent seven-month course, one component is a small group project on various aspects of patient care, organized medicine, or advocacy. Interestingly, every year, one group does a project on physician burnout, even if that topic is not always on the list of curriculum choices. This occurrence suggests that if our physician leaders are wrestling with the topic of burnout year after year, many of the rest of us are grappling with it as well. Knowing we're suffering, naming the problem, writing editorials, and meeting in groups has made little dent in our day-to-day experience, however.

Though physician burnout may abound and can be attributed to multiple factors, naming this syndrome without proposing tangible solutions, or suggesting that relief can come only if systems change simply adds to our feelings of powerlessness. Friends, we cannot wallow in misery, waiting for institutional or government-led transformation any longer. Although we wholeheartedly agree that systems urgently need overhaul, we know the responsibility to improve our health and happiness—and those of our colleagues, patients, and profession—lies squarely within our own hands. With the ideas presented in this book, we hope to empower you to look honestly at your own life and make the necessary course corrections to reframe the vision that led you off track. As each one of us steps off the hamster wheel and revives our alignment, our passion, and our dedication to the values that originally led us to medicine, we can heal our profession entirely and show others a path to relief. Let's get started!

1.

TIME-VALUES MISMATCH

Whatever you can do or dream you can, begin it.
Boldness has genius, power, and magic in it.

—Goethe

After several years of thrashing in all directions, including almost giving up medicine to become a dog groomer (seriously, I actually enrolled in a training program before my plans were derailed by a minor health scare), we finally came to terms with the big-picture source of dissatisfaction in our lives: If how we spend our time does not match what is truly important to us, we are unhappy. The more we spend our time doing what we value and enjoy, the happier we feel.

Shaun and I first were enlightened by this concept through a personal-development course called the Passion Test, developed by Chris and Janet Atwood. In retrospect, this explanation for our dissatisfaction sounds obvious, yet at the time, neither of us had considered in a structured way what was truly important to us. We were trying desperately to survive the demands of our immediate environment and had no game plan or direction. The concept of spending time doing what we value and enjoy, which has emerged many other times in subsequent lectures and courses, has become the navigation system we use to chart the path of our daily lives. It absolutely changes everything.

There are many techniques you can use to clarify your personal values, but the one we use most often involves brainstorming what your *optimal or ideal* life might include. When I first did this exercise, the only item I could think of read something like "In my envisioned perfect life, I get restful sleep every night, without a pager or phone next to my head." I was so utterly exhausted at the time that nothing seemed as important as uninterrupted sleep.

Over the years, the list of what is truly and uniquely important to me has undergone multiple revisions, extending beyond basic needs such as sleep and into more expansive concepts. At present, my personal core-values list includes the following:

1. Enjoy time in nature every day

2. Share meaningful relationships

3. Be dedicated to restorative self-care

4. Live my daily life in a way that genuinely reflects the spiritual paradigm I believe in

5. Support myself and others in finding ways to live with peace and ease

6. Be absolutely financially free

Shaun's list includes the following:

1. Be well rested

2. Live intentionally

3. Enjoy meaningful relationships with family and friends

4. Be fit, strong, and healthy

5. Spend time in prayer, reflection, or personal development every day

6. Use my gifts and skills to benefit humankind

7. Work with energetic, positive, like-minded people

Through mentoring friends and colleagues over the years in clarifying their values, we have found that while some themes are fairly common, others are very individualized. We have seen lists that include eating delicious food, playing piano in Carnegie Hall, being a Supreme Court justice, living in a beach house with an ocean view, golfing every day in Hawaii, having great sex, developing a spiritual practice, and spending time with family. There is no limit to what you can include on your list; the only caveat is that you take the time to sit down and actually consider what is important to you. Once you have a sense of what matters, you can then use this as a guide to help you determine how to spend your time in a meaningful way.

Take my list, for example, which has enjoying time in nature at the very top. When I originally settled on my current list, I was basically spending seven days a week under fluorescent lighting in the hospital, arriving and leaving in the dark. My time outdoors mostly involved walking my dog around the neighborhood and scurrying from my car to the door in the hospital parking lot. Of course, the stressful aspects of my job, including endless documentation, were sucking the life out of me; however, the larger portion of my unhappiness was directly related to not enjoying time outside. Once I started hiking every Tuesday with my best friend, even when nothing else changed, my life seemed suddenly easier and more manageable.

Shaun says, "I came to realize I was over-committed and had said yes to too many committee obligations out of a sense of responsibility, rather than making well-thought-out choices to be involved. Once I had completed the values-clarification process, I evaluated every committee, appointed position, and teaching obligation I had taken on and questioned whether they were moving me toward or away from my ideal life. Those that were moving in the direction of how I wanted to live remained, and the others were resigned or phased out. I also reviewed things I had stopped doing that at one time had brought me great joy, including weekly dance classes and monthly scrapbooking with friends. I had stopped doing these things because I was overextended in other areas that needed to be reevaluated. What a difference it made to give up the things that brought me no joy, and add the things that did! When how you want to live aligns with how you are actually living, every aspect of life is positively affected."

Dissatisfaction related to time-values mismatch also applies directly to patient care. We heard one physician describe her frustration in treating patients with handfuls of antidepressants when she felt that the patients would additionally benefit from holistic and nutritional therapies. Time constraints in her schedule, however, allowed her only to prescribe medications and left little room for detailed discussion of the non-pharmaceutical strategies she believed were equally important. Naturally, this doctor was unhappy at work because she was spending much of her time treating patients in a way that was not congruent with her values pertaining to providing care.

Take a moment now to consider the following questions.

What are your core values?

What is truly important to you?

How wide is the gap between what you value and how you spend your time?

As you make decisions going forward, could you choose a course that is more aligned with what is important to you?

If the concept of making a values list does not appeal to you, consider what you would do if you had a billion dollars (yes, *billion*, with a B) in your bank account, or answer the question "What sounds fun?" Both of these exercises will get you in the vicinity of what's truly important to you. Once you have something on paper, ask yourself, "How can I have some component of this right now?" For example, if you feel that living anonymously on a yacht sounds fun, that may indicate that you are exhausted and overextended, that you love boating, or both. What could you do starting tomorrow to rearrange your schedule to get more rest, to resign from a committee or project that doesn't inspire you, or to plan a trip to the ocean? As you make choices going forward, continue to deliberately honor what is important to you, and slowly, the joy will creep back into your life.

What you can do to revive your situation:

1. Clarify your own personal values using introspective questions such as What does my ideal life look like? What would I do if I had a billion dollars? What sounds fun? What would I do if I were not a healthcare professional? If I could start life over completely, what would I do differently?

2. Once you have your true values clarified, compare how you are currently spending your time to what you have determined to be important to you. The level of personal distress you currently feel is likely related to the size of the gap you just identified.

3. Start taking small steps in the direction of your core values.

4. Enlist the help of a coach or mentor to help you if you become stuck. I made great progress working with Heather Fork, MD, CPCC, at the Doctor's Crossing; Shaun had a good experience with Wendy Samson at FutureSYNC International; and we both benefited greatly from Byron Katie's The Work, and, The Passion Test book and seminars from Chris and Janet Atwood.

5. Recognize that improving your life is not about goading your employer into giving you what you want, but rather about taking responsibility for yourself and your happiness and collaborating with your employer to create improvements.

What organizations can do to support providers and improve engagement:

1. Host seminars, host grand rounds, and/or hire coaches who help providers, managers, and administrators clarify their values.

2. Support employees in living lives that align with their values at work and out of the office by encouraging personal and professional development.

3. Collaborate with providers and other employees to develop a set of *shared* workplace values and goals. This will dramatically improve engagement, as individuals more readily support initiatives that they are involved in creating.

4. Recognize that supporting providers is not about manipulating your employees into compliance with your agenda, but rather about creating a collaborative team around a shared vision.

2.

FALSE EXPECTATIONS

Never wish life were easier, wish you were better.

—Jim Rohn

How often do you feel that the job you are doing is not the one you signed up for? Maybe we're old-school, but we cannot recall sitting in medical-school histology class dreaming of days when we would be worried about money, spend weekends and vacations on documentation, fight patients over incorrect Google diagnoses, or work harder to meet arbitrary compliance mandates than to improve someone's quality of life. We envisioned careers with challenges in discovering diagnoses and creating just the right treatment plan. We imagined complicated surgeries, late nights delivering babies, collegiate camaraderie, and, most of all, feeling appreciated. Financial concerns weren't on our radar, nor were computers, lawsuits, or ICD-10. We assumed that the end of our training signaled the end of our struggling—but, wow, were we wrong in our thinking!

In looking closely at the issues troubling us and other physicians today, we see that many of those challenges seem to stem from the gap between what we imagined and what is actually happening. Everywhere we turn, we find ourselves plagued by the *shoulds* and *shouldn'ts*: We should have more time to interview patients. We should spend more time actually treating patients than we do on documentation. We should get to sleep at night. We shouldn't be sued for something that isn't our fault. We shouldn't be worried about money. We shouldn't have to click boxes for meaningful use, select exactly the right code for billing, or track work relative value units (RVUs). We shouldn't have to comply with arbitrary accreditation rules. We shouldn't have to deal with doctor shaming or patient-satisfaction scores that rely on pain control only to be faulted for causing the epidemic of prescription drug abuse. We shouldn't have to catch up on paperwork during dinner or while on vacation. We shouldn't have to argue with patients over self-diagnoses of systemic Candida or whether they can safely give birth underwater. Our administration and our government should be more supportive. We shouldn't have to work eighty hours a week. We should feel happy in our chosen profession. Things simply shouldn't be this difficult.

Every one of us likely struggled a bit with passing exams, getting accepted into medical school, or navigating the challenges of residency, but most of us assumed that things would improve personally, professionally, and financially once we began as attending physicians. Indeed, the clinical care ratcheted down from 80–100 hours to 40–60 hours per week, yet the paperwork caught us off guard. Our incomes skyrocketed, but so did our debts, and hours spent covering call in training became hours chained to our computers as attending physicians. Also gone were the days of resident camaraderie as we found ourselves working alone.

We'd had no insight into the fact that more than half of our postgraduate time would be spent on nonclinical busywork, yet by then we were trapped. To do what we love—serving humanity through medicine—we had to comply. We had to learn how to navigate EMR, chart for a jury, complete disability paperwork, document for insurance payments, select diagnosis codes so our hospitals get paid, designate inpatients, read patient blogs for advice, schedule surgery without speaking to an actual human, complete applications for insurance panels, check boxes for meaningful use, track work RVUs, earn enough continuing medical education (CME) to comply with insurance requirements, maintain our credentials, and stay certified with entities such as Neonatal Resuscitation Program (NRP), Advanced Cardiac Life Support (ACLS), fetal heart monitoring, and our professional organizations. *This is not what we signed up to do!* Is it any surprise, then, that a few years into this debacle, physicians find themselves frustrated, irritable, unfulfilled, and suffering from burnout?

To practice medicine in America, however, we must face these facts: Less than half of our time will be spent on direct patient care; nonsensical requirements abound; documentation is not going away; and patients are reading the Internet. More and more, we will be measured by our degree of compliance with patient requests, hospital policies, nursing protocols, and governing-body criteria rather than by the quality of care we provide or the compassion in our hearts. In fact, we believe it is only because of our tremendous inherent compassion that any of us still show up to work in this treacherous environment.

More and more, we will be measured by our degree of compliance with patient requests, hospital policies, nursing protocols, and governing-body criteria rather than by the quality of care we provide or the compassion in our hearts.

Going forward, the path to relief comes not from expecting the system to change or the busywork to lessen but from standing firmly on the status quo and looking inward from there. Ranting about the ridiculousness of our system, the haphazard use of physician resources, or the fact that most of our time is spent wasted yields only frustration and angst. Instead, we must ask ourselves these questions truthfully: Do I love clinical care enough to continue working in this environment just as it is? Can I personally structure my life to reduce my involvement in busywork? How can I find joy in the midst of these challenges? Can I streamline my EMR to autofill templates and eliminate duplications?

We must realize that in working, we are no longer exchanging our expertise for money in a way that uniformly benefits humanity but are instead trading hours of our lives for dollars in a system that has little appreciation for our value and that preferentially treats patients who know how to navigate its particulars.

As I have stopped resisting the busywork, released my grip on MD as my identity (see chapter 3), and embraced the future of my core values (see chapter 1), I have found the experience of medical practice to be much less distressing. I have clear expectations that less than half of my time will be spent in clinic or surgery and that the system cares more about how well I click boxes than how well I treat patients. Nevertheless, I have committed myself to taking care of my patients in a way that is personally acceptable to me, reflects my best ability, and offers the most compassion within the confines of the matrix I work in.

We agree wholeheartedly that modern medicine urgently needs change, but we believe that the immediate challenge facing us is to not waste energy fighting the system but to creatively and joyfully provide outstanding care amid this confusion.

Shaun says, "While I still feel frustrated when, for example, I have to draft multiple letters to an insurance company to defend continuing a medication that a patient has been stable on for years, I have stopped fighting the idea that this type of work is not part of my job as a physician. I have embraced the challenging task of finding ways to provide excellent care within the sometimes nonsensical structure of modern healthcare."

We agree wholeheartedly that modern medicine urgently needs change, but we believe that the immediate challenge facing us is to not waste energy fighting the system but to creatively and joyfully provide outstanding care amid this confusion. If we decide to continue our medical work in the American hospital-employed, insurance-based system, we can find fulfillment only to the extent that we can release our grip on the shoulds, reframe our expectations, and appreciate ourselves for the excellent care we provide.

What you can do to revive your situation:

1. Write down exactly what you expected from your medical career.

2. As you go through a week in your practice, track every frustration you encounter and list the way you think it ideally should be instead.

3. Look at your list and ask yourself if anything there will realistically change in the foreseeable future. If so, celebrate! If not, don't waste another ounce of your energy on expecting impossible changes; instead, get to work finding creative ways to function peacefully within your existing situation. Alternatively, if you feel the limitations are intolerably burdensome, use your energy to start looking for a new employer or career.

4. Look at your list and ask yourself if there is anything you can do to move things toward your ideal vision. If so, take action on those items you have some control over.

5. Share your success stories with others.

What organizations can do to support providers and improve engagement:

1. Take an honest, introspective look at how you truly view providers. Is your organization expecting providers to do something specific, to perform in certain ways, or to advance your financial agenda? Are these expectations even in the ballpark of what your providers understand their responsibilities to be?

2. Proactively support your providers in their nonclinical requirements. Make every effort to help providers optimize EMR use, streamline workflow, and have adequate staff and appropriate supplies available in patient-care areas.

3. Proactively support your providers with data entry and clerical work. Hiring clerical staff to enter orders, scribe notes, complete insurance and disability forms, type letters, and the like will free up clinicians to spend more of their time seeing patients and doing procedures, which improves patient access, revenue for the organization, and physician satisfaction. Many providers are reluctant to increase their patient loads because they know that every hour of face-to-face patient care means two hours of unpaid busywork carved out of their evenings and weekends.

Many providers are reluctant to increase their patient loads because they know that every hour of face-to-face patient care means two hours of unpaid busywork carved out of their evenings and weekends.

3.

IDENTITY CRISIS

The practice of forgiveness is our most important contribution to the healing of the world.

—Marianne Williamson

It's insanity, really. We strive ridiculously hard to get MD after our names, yet once listed there, the letters become bubble gum stuck to our sneakers: awesome at first, then a terrible mess. Once we become Doctor So-and-so, it's as if we can no longer see the world through the lens of humanity and are stuck with MD goggles clouding our view. Instead of considering what sounds fun or seeing a buffet of alternatives, we limit ourselves with thoughts such as these:

I can't become an Uber driver; I'm a doctor!

I can't live in a trailer; I'm a doctor!

I can't attend pole-dancing class; I'm a doctor!

I can't be a stay-at-home mom; I'm a doctor!

I can't start a network marketing business; I'm a doctor!

I can't just quit; I'm a doctor!

What about my patients, my reputation, and my 401K?

What will my family or my partners tell people now—that I used to be a respectable doctor but I couldn't hack it and now I'm a quitter?

If we step out of line, we feel guilty and accountable to society, the mentors who trained us, loved ones whose graduations and funerals we missed because we were working, our families who spent nights alone with the kids while we were on call, and the patients we could be treating if we continued our profession. We take ourselves way too seriously. Even enjoying vacation for a week or two is impossible as we worry that our partners will crumble, our patients will suffer, and we will return to more chaos than we left.

Guess what? The world absolutely turns without us. Patients find treatment, administrators find solutions, and, though we would like to believe otherwise, we are, to some degree, expendable.

At the peak of my personal dissatisfaction with clinical medicine, I felt irreparably trapped. I looked around and saw my only marketable skill to be obstetrics and gynecology; everywhere I turned, I felt disappointed. How could a career I had fought tooth and nail to achieve bring me this much distress, and how could I walk away and disappoint everyone who had helped me? Abandoning medicine felt like chopping off my own arm, yet continuing felt like absolute torture. Who would I be if I weren't a doctor, yet how could I live with myself if I stayed?

Ultimately, with the help of a coach and a few months off, I explored different options, including attending massage school, trying locum tenens, and traveling to South Sudan with Médecins Sans Frontières/Doctors Without Borders (MSF). During my time away, I remembered what I loved about clinical medicine, and I also reengaged the parts of myself that had gotten lost in single-minded dedication to my degree. I remembered that I love writing, speaking, philosophy, whales, trail running, travel, and massage.

Once I broke up with my identity as a doctor and engaged my identity as a human, the situation became much more manageable.

Eventually, I returned to medical practice, but with equal attention to the rest of my being. I recognized that time spent trail running with friends is equally important as performing a vaginal hysterectomy or delivering a baby. Once I broke up with my identity as a doctor and engaged my identity as a human, the situation became much more manageable. Nothing had changed in my work environment; all the same challenges remained, but because I no longer attached my identity to doctoring and instead dedicated myself to enjoying a fulfilling life (doctor or not), the same hassles didn't seem so severe.

Shaun says, "I broke up with my degree in the traditional sense and joined forces with it as a tool to promote a new business and engage in meaningful global projects. In exploring my options, I discovered I loved coaching and promoting health and wellness as much as anything specifically related to western medical practice. I also discovered my passion for women's health from a global perspective and linked arms with Save the Mothers. In these contexts, my MD degree offered great insight and credibility in launching a network marketing business and in contributing to a meaningful international organization, and I have used my clinical expertise to move forward in these venues."

The main point here is that if *MD* feels like a noose around your neck securing you indefinitely to clinical practice, loosen the knot and throw out the rope. You can change careers altogether, modify your circumstance, or use your degree to propel yourself forward in another endeavor. The only thing truly revealing about those letters is that you are dedicated and tenacious in achieving a goal. At one point, your goal was an MD degree, and you got there. Now, however, your goal may be different. You can use your perseverance to improve your life, enhance your joy, or change direction completely.

Don't ask yourself only how you can use your medical training to earn an equivalent salary outside of clinical practice. Also ask yourself what sounds fun and what you would do if you were not a doctor. As a human being living on this earth, how would you like to spend your remaining time?

So, choose to continue in medicine if you love it, and if you don't, rearrange your situation to revive the joy, or choose to pursue something else. People change careers all the time, and you have the option and *permission* to choose any career you prefer. Don't ask yourself only how you can use your medical training to earn an equivalent salary outside of clinical practice. Also ask yourself what sounds fun and what you would do if you were not a doctor. As a human being living on this earth, how would you like to spend your remaining time?

If you originally felt drawn to clinical practice by a compelling force from a young age, then it is likely your future holds ongoing contribution through medicine. If you enjoy patient care but struggle with logistics, there is a good chance that rearranging your schedule or adding a scribe will bring the relief you desire. If, however, you're miserable all around and feel held hostage by your medical degree, by all means, move on despite it. (We know of one young doctor who successfully traded the practice of medicine for organic farming and of another who scrapped medicine to open a restaurant.) Your intelligence and determination were clearly fierce enough for you to earn your MD in the first place, and that same tenacity can be redirected toward a more rewarding or enjoyable pursuit.

What's truly stopping you? Is it the idea that doctors don't create surfboards, or that doctors should work for at least twenty years before retiring? Maybe it's your family's expectation that you fulfill a medical legacy.

Chances are, the culprit is intimately tied to your identification with the letters MD rather than to a genuine barrier.

If it's truly time for you to pursue a different career, realize that you have likely already helped hundreds of patients and that may be exactly enough.

What you can do to revive your situation:

1. Ask yourself what you would do if you were not a doctor.

2. Ask yourself, "As a human being living on this earth, how would I like to spend my remaining time?" Your answer may or may not include medical practice. If it does, embrace your choice wholeheartedly! If not, give yourself permission to make a change even if it means having a lower income, returning to school, or moving out of town. You had the tenacity to survive pre-med, medical school, and residency, and you can use that same skill set to confidently reinvent yourself if needed.

3. If you want to see how tightly you are tied to the letters after your name, attend a conference or social event and introduce yourself without giving away your profession. Evaluate how hard or easy this is for you.

4. Make a list of exactly what's distressing you about your medical work. Evaluate how much of that list is related to the logistics of your job and how much is tied to your inherent contribution through medicine. If the listed items are primarily logistical, how can you decrease those hassles? If you can't eliminate the hassles, how can you reduce your stress regarding them?

5. Honor the contributions you have already made. If it's truly time for you to pursue a different career, realize that you have likely already helped hundreds of patients and that may be exactly enough.

6. Resist the temptation to compare yourself to doctors who have been in practice longer than you or who seem to be faring better than you.

7. Realize that you are not obligated to contribute to society specifically through medicine, even if that's where you started. You may have hundreds of other as-yet-untapped gifts and talents to share with the world.

8. Realize that you don't have to quit. If you love your identity as a physician and you feel passionate about the clinical practice of medicine, you can find a way to practice that is joyful and not depleting. Make your own rearrangements, contact us for help, or work with a coach or a mentor to get reoriented to a career you enjoy.

If you love your identity as a physician and you feel passionate about the clinical practice of medicine, you can find a way to practice that is joyful and not depleting.

4.

ISOLATION

I saw an angel in the stone and carved to set it free.

—Michelangelo

H ave you ever impulsively fantasized about driving your car off the road or being diagnosed with a rapidly terminal illness?

Don't worry; if you have, you're not alone and you're not crazy. Many of us have had similar thoughts.

Tragically, I have known two competent and well-liked providers who killed themselves, one still in training and one after years on the job. The first was found dead in a call room from overdose, the second in his home from a self-inflicted gunshot wound. Both shocked their respective communities, as none of us knew they were even slightly distressed. They came to work on time, well-dressed and smiling, discussed weekend events, and shared photos of family and pets. They described stories from their pasts, told of plans for their futures, and were integral parts of their clinical teams. News of their deaths was unfathomable to us, based on their characters we had come to know on the job. These were not curmudgeonly souls hanging on by a thread but pleasant, healthy, intelligent, seemingly happy-go-lucky young people in the prime of their lives. What happened?

In the depths of crisis, suicide, although misguided, seems to effectively cancel our personal and professional responsibilities, and conceals our personal failures.

The statistic that more than 400 physicians commit suicide annually is disturbing but hardly surprising. Once, a beloved physician confessed to me that she felt ending her own life was "the only respectable way out." Any provider who ever secretly prayed for a terminal illness or wished quietly to get hit by a bus understands her sentiments exactly. From the outside, we doctors seem to have it all: respect, money, skills, status, and job security. Whenever I've mentioned feeling distressed or unhappy to a person outside of clinical medicine, I've been met with a look that seems to say, "Seriously, you're rich and you're respected. What do you have to complain about?" and reminds me that I'm in dangerous territory. While outsiders admire us, we can feel trapped by responsibility, burdened by expectations, powerless, and isolated, especially from colleagues and family.

In the depths of crisis, suicide, although misguided, seems to effectively cancel our personal and professional responsibilities, and conceals our personal failures. It liberates doctors from pending lawsuits, the obligation to treat demanding or difficult patients, unfinished documentation, relentless administrative duties, and unmanageable debt. It means never having to tell another patient that they've miscarried, the biopsy results show cancer, or the paralysis is permanent. Simply ceasing to exist also frees us from facing colleagues who would possibly sneer, "He just couldn't handle it," and the perceived societal humiliation we would endure if we voluntarily gave up our medical practice. Unfortunately, suicide also conveys the magnitude of our invisible pain to a world that doesn't understand how deeply we sometimes suffer.

Isolation is a dangerous beast. We may be surrounded by patients, coworkers, family, and friends but have exactly zero trusted confidants with whom to share our true experiences. It can feel like there's *no one to talk to*. If we tell our colleagues the extent of our suffering, at best, they may worry we're cracking up and we won't be able to pull our weight clinically, then pass us over for referrals and surgery. We fear that, at worst, they might report us to administration or to the medical board as unfit for duty, or gossip of our "weakness" to other clinicians. If we seek professional help, we worry not only about confidentiality and being recognized by our patients as we sit in community waiting rooms, but also about being labeled with blacklisted diagnoses. Unfortunately, a formal diagnosis of major depression or other mental illness can mean rejection for disability, health, or life insurance policies. It can also rear its ugly head to undermine our credibility in court should we find ourselves on the stand.

I learned my lesson about this in residency. At the time, I briefly pursued counseling for distress triggered by a breakup with my boyfriend coinciding with some family issues. Several years later, I was rejected for a disability insurance policy based on my self-reported history of counseling and was advised that I would be eligible for the policy in five years—as long as I didn't seek care in the interim. Naturally, if I felt troubled thereafter, I didn't tell anyone and didn't seek counseling even when I knew it would help. I remember during my lowest points desperately racking my brain for even one person to call who could help me confidentially process my feelings without a potentially punitive outcome. Ultimately, I found relief with an out-of-state coach whom I could speak with by phone. This person could relate to both my logistical and emotional challenges and helped me brainstorm solutions without fear of humiliation or reproach.

Shaun notes, "When I was deepest in the grip of burnout, I didn't even know what was happening; I couldn't have named it. All I knew is that I felt miserable and I couldn't fix it. There were certainly times I fleetingly thought to myself while driving, 'If I swerved off this bridge right now, my suffering would instantly cease.' Reflecting on those thoughts now brings tears to my eyes, recalling how deeply I was hurting, and yet no one knew. My husband was aware that I was overwhelmed, but as I was a strong, independent woman, he assumed I'd get things sorted out. I had never told anyone about those thoughts until Melissa and I began weekly tea-time discussions and I realized I had been feeling depressed for more than a year but carrying on as though everything were fine. Having an honest conversation with a trusted friend helped me turn things around. Isolation in this profession is a serious problem and something we must find the courage to discuss openly."

Physician suicide and distress are real phenomena, and for every provider who ends his or her life, hundreds of others are living on edge.

The bottom line is this: Physician suicide and distress are real phenomena, and for every provider who ends his or her life, hundreds of others are living on edge. That their outwardly joyful demeanor is showcased while their compassion for others prevents them from pulling the trigger does not mean they are not suffering deeply. At a conference, one beautiful and seemingly high-spirited woman confided to me that she had felt so unimaginably awful the night before our conversation that she had considered ending her life. She had a detailed plan and had even brought the relevant drugs to the conference hotel. She had decided not to go through with her plan because she didn't want to traumatize the housekeeping staff who would find her body in the bathroom or her husband, who would receive the call from police that she had died.

So, how can we help ourselves here? Does isolation lead to burnout, which leads to depression? Does depression lead to isolation, which leads to burnout? Or does burnout lead to isolation, which then leads to depression? Does the etiologic chain even matter? Ultimately, isolation is a serious problem that appears in the personal and professional lives even of those who are not depressed. With the camaraderie of medical school and residency behind us, we often find ourselves alone in our offices, call rooms, and the operating room. We type our charts in deserted clinics and consult online libraries for patient-care suggestions, spending more time facing computers than humans. At home, we find relief in alcohol or prescriptions, or in busyness, as nonmedical spouses cannot possibly understand what we feel. We scurry from patient to patient, meeting to meeting, home to office, exchanging small talk in passing but never carving out time or mustering the courage for meaningful conversations with like-minded colleagues.

If we expect to revive ourselves from the so-called burnout epidemic and reduce the horrifying tragedy of suicide felling doctors nationwide, we must commit to coming out of our isolationist shells and genuinely connecting with others. This can be tackled with the logistical strategies listed at the end of this chapter, though the most critical components are internal. They include finding the courage to expose our vulnerabilities, taking the time and initiative to truly reach out to our colleagues, destigmatizing depression for everyone, and, most importantly, rejecting the shame we feel at not always being able to gracefully handle the personal and professional responsibilities we've fought so hard to obtain.

Only through mutual collaboration and shared vulnerability will we recognize our common plight, find like-minded partners with whom to process our thoughts, and come to a common understanding. In sharing our experiences with others, we reveal the ubiquitous nature of our suffering, and instead of feeding the "no one understands me, this is just too much, I can't possibly continue" mindset, we can focus our attention on healing.

What you can do to revive your situation:

1. Make a pact with a colleague or family member that neither one of you will resort to suicide, no matter what. In my darkest moments, I'm always reminded of a promise my sister and I made to each other in our twenties, and though I may wish to vaporize myself in the moment, I know I would never violate our pact.

2. Get addicted to healthy self-care behaviors instead of numbing behaviors such as alcohol.

3. Share your true feelings with someone, such as a trusted colleague in another profession, a counselor, a coach, or someone on an anonymous hotline.

4. Focus on personal development through workshops, classes, books, or webinars.

5. Develop a spiritual practice.

6. Create margin by booking unscheduled time into your life for relief.

7. Relinquish responsibilities that are not joyful: Resign from committees; reduce your work schedule; cancel extracurricular activities that steal your time and don't bring fulfillment.

8. Have regular "tea time" with a trusted friend and use that time to speak openly with each other.

9. Revisit the time-values mismatch exercise (chapter 1) and realign how you spend your time with what is important to you.

10. Have meaningful conversations. Go ahead and ask people questions that you really want to know the answers to, such as "Are you feeling distressed by your career? Are you happy in your marriage? Do you truly feel joyful or happy? What do you think about most of the time? Do you believe in God? What mistakes have you made? What regrets do you have? How has your medical career affected your relationships and your health? In what way have your decisions hurt your patients, your family, your well-being?" This practice will help you find people you can genuinely reveal yourself to.

11. Attend conferences with like-minded professionals so you can mingle with others who understand what you are experiencing. (We first met the most empathetic doctors at an event by SEAK called Non-Clinical Careers for Physicians conference.)

What organizations can do to support providers and improve engagement:

1. Recognize that physician burnout is a real phenomenon affecting providers in your organization. Take this topic seriously.

2. Offer regular presentations on recognizing, preventing, and addressing provider burnout, depression, and suicide.

3. Destigmatize depression and mental health issues among providers by not treating them punitively if they reach out for help.

4. Host regular forums in which provider distress and burnout are discussed freely among physicians and relevant solutions are brainstormed and implemented.

5. Offer free, confidential off-site or phone counseling to providers that they can access themselves without being formally or informally blacklisted.

6. Develop and share transparent policies that detail exactly what happens to providers who seek help for major depression or addiction, and how receiving treatment will or will not affect their careers or employment.

7. Really listen to providers when they express what they need to function best in their clinics and on the ward. For example, having a scribe, pairing with a different nurse, or rearranging schedules could mean the difference between a provider who is exasperated and one who has manageable stress.

8. Support policies that allow providers to take appropriate self-care measures, such as adequate sleep, exercise, nutrition, and vacation.

9. Support provider well-being directly with an on-site counselor, nutritious meal options, gym memberships, corporate massage, and the like.

10. Have formal debriefing processes after traumas, deaths, and poor outcomes that include eliciting how providers feel about what happened and giving them relevant tools to process and move through those emotions.

11. Offer regular seminars that acknowledge provider distress, and offer tools to providers that help them navigate the emotional complexity of their profession.

12. Bring in mediators to help providers or offices with interpersonal problems work together more collegially.

13. Give offices annual monetary and time budgets to use specifically for social outings, retreats, and/or team-building events.

14. Offer providers budgets to be used only for coaching or personal development separate from CME, and encourage them to use it. Bring in your own coaches, if you prefer. This eliminates the stigma of counseling yet still allows individuals to address many of their personal, financial, and workplace frustrations in a nonthreatening way. Encourage all providers to participate—not just those perceived to be struggling or burned out—so no one feels targeted. Showcase the success of participants thereafter if they are willing to publicly share a piece of their story.

5.

FEELING UNDERVALUED

Change the way you look at things, and the things you look at change.

—Wayne Dyer

"I take care of myself reasonably well and I enjoy taking care of patients, but overall, I just don't feel valued."

As we interviewed physicians over the past few years, our hearts broke, as we heard this from almost every single one. What is it about the current state of affairs that has left such exceptional giving, compassionate, hardworking, and dedicated people feeling undervalued, insignificant, and as if our contributions are meaningless?

Proposed theories suggest decreased appreciation from patients who want to entirely direct their own care, the influence of direct-to-consumer prescription advertising, organizations that employ us as expendable workers ("Comply with our rules, or you're out"), greater interaction with computers than with people, systems that stress the importance of computer documentation over quality patient care, perpetual paper cuts (see chapter 12), constant threat of lawsuits regardless of quality of care provided, and pageantry of report cards based on arbitrary patient-satisfaction scores.

Our work feels meaningless because *much of it is!*

Although these may all contribute greatly to our overall sense of feeling unimportant, we propose that at the heart of the issue, our work feels meaningless because *much of it is!* Systems have spiraled entirely out of control, forgetting the human professionals who actually meet their patients face-to-face. To survive in modern medicine, providers must shrink their thinking to accommodate multiple system parameters while interacting with patients, many of whom are attached to their doctors only as long as they get immediate appointments or the prescriptions they saw on TV. We love our patients and have dedicated our careers to partnering with them to live healthier lives; however, much of this process is becoming unmanageable.

In modern healthcare, instead of having our professional medical opinions sought after, we are asked to comply with standard hospital, nursing, and organizational protocols, many of which don't actually apply to any individual patient. Have you gotten a call from your local pharmacy saying you prescribed the "wrong" medication and that policy dictates you must change it, regardless of your reasoning? There goes your medical decision making. What about Shaun's favorite: the fax from an insurance company questioning why she prescribed a medication that her patient had been stable on for years instead of prescribing the medication on their standard formulary? Have you become an expert at debating the esteemed Dr. Google, who obviously has greater diagnostic skills than you? Have you found yourself negotiating with a patient about whether she does in fact have a new diagnosis of diabetes with a fasting glucose of 200 despite the fact that she is vegetarian and does hot yoga every day? Have you been unable to schedule a medically indicated procedure, surgery, or labor induction because of "staffing issues"? How often do you show up to clinic and discover patients you never agreed to see scheduled through your lunch break or tacked on to the end of your day? These situations crop up repeatedly in hospitals and communities of all sizes and, unfortunately, have become the norm for most healthcare professionals.

Similarly, patients now approach us to fill prescriptions for medications they saw in ads, to test for conditions their neighbors believe they have, or to complete forms giving them time off work regardless of medical necessity. If their insurance happens to change, so does their loyalty. "What, you don't have an appointment available today for my 'emergency' annual wellness exam even though you've been my doctor for years? I guess I'll just call someone else." It seems that to achieve excellent patient satisfaction, we must ignore the primary tenets of clinical medicine and become Pez dispensers for pharmaceuticals, fill in forms as some patients dictate, and accommodate unnecessary appointments on client demand. This combination of system restrictions and patient mandates has all but reduced us to robots. Again, *our work feels meaningless because much of it is.*

Of course, not all patients behave in this manner. Some are so unfathomably loyal, so attached, so committed to their providers that they refuse to see anyone else. This creates an opposite problem, wherein the patient feels rejected when his or her usual physician is unavailable, and the provider feels solely responsible for that individual's care. The burden of keeping all patients happy by not only attending to their health, but also meeting their demands as above or their emotional need for consistency is impossible. We spend more time trying to figure out means to pacify people than we do collaborating with them on improving their well-being. It's exhausting.

A physician I spoke with regarding working conditions in South Sudan told me, "I never would have imagined wanting to work in a third world country; however, hearing you describe the interesting surgical cases and the patients there, I'm really drawn to it. It sounds mentally stimulating and personally rewarding to operate in those conditions on such unique cases. It must have been fun to practice actual clinical medicine again. Your experience sounds so much different from my daily practice, which is essentially data entry, recertification, and trying to please everyone around me. I feel I've been reduced to performing tasks an eighth-grader could easily handle, and there is almost no true clinical medicine in my career anymore."

So how do we recover? It seems unlikely that we will reclaim our autonomy any time soon from many of our patients, our hospitals, our accrediting bodies, or our government. Do we continue to be reduced to smaller and smaller versions of ourselves, to imprison our creative thinking more and more, to spend greater amounts of our time clicking boxes and acting as Pez dispensers instead of actually contributing through true clinical medicine? Many of us feel like invisible puppets already, so how can we free ourselves from this imposed confinement?

One thing is clear: No one is about to ride in on a white horse and save us. We will not get an email next week stating that documentation is optional, patient-satisfaction scores have been abolished, and we no longer need to preauthorize indicated medications or surgeries through insurance. Our hospital administrators are not going to waltz through the office on Monday morning and declare that we no longer have to complete the online malpractice module or speak to the accreditation surveyor. Patients will not forget Google, and big pharma is not about to stop directly promoting its drugs. We love our patients but their demands are here to stay as well, whether they're about available appointments or pharmaceuticals, and immediate reinstatement of physicians as actual healthcare providers is not likely to happen any time soon.

We believe modern medicine needs to be urgently overhauled—but if our happiness hinges on waiting for patients or systems to change, we can expect to be miserable for decades.

Don't get us wrong; we believe modern medicine needs to be urgently overhauled—but if our happiness hinges on waiting for patients or systems to change, we can expect to be miserable for decades. Shifting our focus and expectations is absolutely the only way out. As long as we look to our patients, colleagues, hospitals, and scores to determine our value, we are doomed to feeling insignificant. If we disconnect our self-worth from the modern systems that confine our profession and instead find that self-worth elsewhere, our experience can immediately shift. With deliberate attention to inherently valuing ourselves and participating in experiences in which we truly do feel useful, we can begin to remember our worth.

Working in South Sudan absolutely changed my experience of western medical practice at home. In the field, there were no other doctors for hundreds of miles and no other surgeons available who could do a cesarean section. When a patient's life was on the line, if I couldn't diagnose the problem and orchestrate a solution, no one was coming to help me. It was terrifying and also exhilarating to actually use my clinical experience in such a resource-poor setting. The results were immediate; if I chose incorrectly, the patient could die. Instead of worrying about documentation, lawsuits, and protocols, I worried about life and death, literally. Incomprehensibly, patients and families genuinely thanked me for my efforts even when outcomes were poor. In a nutshell, I remembered what it felt like to be a "real doctor" again. Back at home, as a cog in the wheel of modern medicine, I carry that experience of feeling valued inside myself, and it absolutely cannot be stolen. As I now feel inherently valuable as a human, the confines of my modern practice don't feel that bothersome anymore.

For Shaun, "Spending time with people in my network marketing business who are energetic and optimistic, and who see their health and well-being as a personal responsibility, has provided a way to recharge my energy and more easily navigate the perceived negatives at work. Through my business, I provide value to a team of people who in turn provide value to me. There are no boxes to click, no preauthorization, and no bureaucracy. In turning away from medicine as the sole source of my value and giving more weight to my wellness business—and also to my Christian faith and my family—I've come to not take every hassle in my medical career so seriously."

The secret to feeling valued by your employer or your patients is to feel valued within yourself.

Does this mean you have to practice in Africa, turn to religion, or start an outside business to regain some sense of yourself? Of course not. But realize that the secret to feeling valued by your employer or your patients is to feel valued within yourself. The happiest physician we know finds inherent value from God through his spiritual beliefs; I found it through international medical service; and Shaun found it through focusing on an invigorating wellness business, her family, and her faith. Maybe you will tangibly feel your value as a parent, as a musician, through volunteer work, or even through caring for your existing patients with a fresh mindset. Whatever the case, you must look to yourself to see your significance, instead of expecting your significance to be bequeathed by the limited parameters of today's medical-industrial complex.

What you can do to revive your situation:

1. Start valuing yourself and your colleagues. Write a colleague or friend a note of appreciation, or share a word of gratitude with him or her. Let others know how they have positively affected your life. I once received a note from a colleague detailing how I had helped her during an important time; that card always comes to mind when I'm down on myself. In fact, those few heartfelt and genuine sentences have helped me rebound from some of my toughest times, and I value those words immensely.

2. Start viewing yourself as a collaborative medical consultant instead of a revered entity with definitive solutions, and release the idea that patients should be loyal and grateful to you for the care you provide.

3. Instead of brushing off their comments as if they were no big deal, take a moment to celebrate and appreciate yourself when you do receive genuine thanks from patients or other providers.

4. Consider training your patients and your partners in the concept of team-based care. This involves patients coming to an office where they know that a group of people cares for them and that they will not be designated unalterably to one individual provider. Doing so relieves the pressure of responsibility from any one person and places it on the broader base of a team. This strategy is not relevant to physicians who value patient loyalty and derive personal satisfaction from being responsible for a defined patient panel; however, for those who feel burdened as such, a team-based approach can offer relief.

5. Keep a special collection of patient thank-you notes, and read through them when you feel insignificant. I once received a card from a patient I didn't even remember meeting, in which she wrote how our conversation had helped her recover from severe postpartum depression. When I'm feeling down on myself, these words are a lifeline. Clearly, even when we feel we're just going through the motions and our contributions are meaningless, we have no certain knowledge of what effect our interactions actually have on our patients.

6. Look for evidence of your value as you go through your day. We tend to see what we focus on, so begin watching for signs that you are valued by your clients, family, friends, organization, and colleagues.

7. Seek out experiences that personally fulfill you, such as volunteer work, family time, international medicine, yacht racing, writing, or whatever suits you.

8. Learn a new skill or offer a new service line at your hospital, such as cosmetic injections, robotic surgery, functional medicine, or acupuncture.

9. Tap in to your creativity. If you feel stifled, reduced to a data-entry monkey at work, find a creative outlet elsewhere. Learn a musical instrument, a new language, or woodworking; become a yoga instructor; take voice lessons; or do whatever else stimulates your creativity. Release the idea that your medical practice has to be the primary or sole source of intellectual or creative stimulation in your life.

What organizations can do to support providers and improve engagement:

1. Include providers in decisions about their work environment and/or supplies. For example, get providers' input when remodeling or designing new clinics, so the build facilitates their workflow.

2. Communicate clearly and often with providers about your intentions and thought processes. In a perfect world, we want to know our organizations are looking out for our best interests, but even knowing that we are considered in a decision-making process is a great start.

3. Don't simply drop new mandates or implement system changes without input. We heard of one facility that implemented a costly communication-system upgrade with pagers that had only twelve hours of continuous battery life. For physicians who worked more than twelve consecutive hours, this not only was impractical but also revealed how little the administration understood or appreciated its providers. Early input from physicians would have avoided this debacle entirely.

4. Include physicians in decision-making processes across the board. When we are included in decision-making processes, we feel heard, we feel that our opinions are important, organizations can see how their decisions will affect clinicians, and common ground can be reached prior to implementation. Even administration doing something as simple as deciding to lock a door that had previously been unlocked can add to provider distress. For example, Shaun once injured her shoulder while plowing into a formerly unlocked door at full speed when trying to rush a critical pregnant patient to emergency surgery.

5. Consider paying providers for being on night and weekend call, in addition to any production generated during their shifts. This shows that you value our health and time and that you recognize that much of the work we do on call does not generate revenue. Even the act of being readily available and mentally prepared to handle whatever crisis arises at any hour can be extremely taxing. Think how many cups of coffee it takes you to wake up in the morning; now imagine rising from a deep sleep at two AM to—within minutes—revive a dying patient, assess a trauma, or operate emergently without making mistakes.

6. Encourage providers to build programs, to volunteer, and to innovate; then publicly recognize their achievements. You likely have a collection of unbelievably accomplished people right under your nose who will feel valued as you recognize their success. Don't limit the recognition to honoring the highest financial producers or those with five-star ratings from patients. Showcase the coaches, athletes, humanitarians, researchers, educators, polyglots, entrepreneurs, activists, musicians, and artists in your ranks. This not only is great for morale but also can enhance your overall marketing effectiveness and shows that you recognize that actual people, not puppets, work for your organization.

7. Dedicate yourself wholeheartedly to transparency and communication when interacting with providers. It is impossible for providers and administrators to collaborate when they have different agendas and neither group understands or appreciates what the other is trying to accomplish.

6.

NUMBNESS

Between stimulus and response there is a space. In that space is our power to choose our response. In our response lies our growth and our freedom.

—Viktor E. Frankl

I t has been said that depersonalization—meaning feelings of cynicism, apathy, or indifference—is one of the core characteristics of burnout. So how did we, the compassionate folks who persevered through the rigors of education and training for the opportunity to care for people in their most vulnerable moments, lose our ability to feel? How did we become angry and indifferent toward the patients we entrusted ourselves to support? Why have we become incomprehensibly numb, and how can we revive our emotion?

So how did we, the compassionate folks who persevered through the rigors of education and training for the opportunity to care for people in their most vulnerable moments, lose our ability to feel?

Recall for a moment your residency. Were you encouraged to take meal or bathroom breaks on call, or were you ridiculed for weakness when you had to excuse yourself? Were you sent home after working for twenty-four hours to accommodate your personal well-being or because your facility would be fined big bucks if you were caught logging extra hours on the job? Were you taught to cry with your patients as they experienced traumatic events, or to maintain your objectivity and stoically present the facts? Did the debriefing process following a trauma or a bad outcome include how providers felt about the situation, or were only the medical facts of the case and the functionality of the team reviewed?

44

Were you encouraged to feel, show, or address your exhaustion, over-whelm, fear, or frustration? Were you supported or berated in the oper-ating room or on the ward by a more senior provider? When you were taught to deliver bad news, such as a cancer diagnosis, a fetal demise, or the death of a loved one, were you instructed on how to deal with your personal sadness or only the patient's emotions? At the completion of your training, did you feel well prepared to deal with the emotional com-plexities of caring for others? Did you attend even one class on how to support yourself throughout your physically, emotionally, and spiritu-ally taxing profession?

We're guessing that we know the answers. More likely than not, you were expected to care diligently for others when feeling ill or tired, when hypoglycemic, and even when pregnant, until the onset of labor. You were taught how to gracefully comfort patients but not how to soothe yourself. You likely learned over three to five years how to suppress both your biologic signals such as hunger, thirst, exhaustion, and urinary urgency and your emotional inputs of rage, tearfulness, disappointment, and helplessness. You probably received exactly zero instruction on how to navigate the emotional tumultuousness of medical practice.

Naturally, this type of training has a legitimate purpose and extends into the realities of our chosen profession. For example, one night, in adjoin-ing rooms, I took care of a woman with a thirty-nine-week intrauterine demise being induced to deliver her full-term deceased baby while con-currently caring for a woman in labor with a thirty-nine-week healthy baby. Both pregnancies were the couples' first, and both were filled with the dreams and plans of starting a family. As you can imagine, in one room, the tone was unbearably heartbreaking and full of the couple's agony over having lost their child, while in the adjacent room, the atmosphere was of overwhelming excitement. In one room, I handed a tearfully distraught couple a dead baby, and shortly thereafter, in the next, I handed a tearfully overjoyed couple a live child.

Caring for these families required me to keep my emotions at bay and to behave professionally throughout the night, matching my demeanor, back and forth, to each situation. If I had let my true emotion get the best of me, I would have been crying hysterically at the unfairness of life and would have been unable to perform my medical responsibility, which was to bring each child safely into the world without causing harm to the mother. We all know this professional dance. How many times have we dealt with medical tragedies such as this or emergencies in which, while feeling devastated or terrified, we stuff those sensations away so we can function intellectually and implement critical decisions? Over time we become so unbelievably skilled at suppressing emotion that we lose touch with the signal completely.

Over time we become so unbelievably skilled at suppressing emotion that we lose touch with the signal completely.

Similarly, we often witness extreme situations and are subsequently plagued by relativism. We have seen blood pouring off beds onto the floor, patients coding and dying, children cachectic with metastatic cancer, bones protruding from limbs, and full-term intrauterine death. Those of us who have worked overseas have seen extreme malnutrition, famine, fistula, and childhood death from preventable diseases or simple lack of clean water. Then, in modern clinics, we come face-to-face with patients inconsolable over tiny drops of blood shed, the inability to lose the last five pounds, almost-indiscernible acne, an imperceptible bruise, an intermittent eye twitch, or self-reported PTSD from a birth perceived to be traumatic because Pitocin was required when not on the delivery plan.

Naturally, these issues are distressing and scary to those who are experiencing them, but in comparison to the catastrophes that many health-care professionals have witnessed, they sometimes barely register with us. It is therefore relatively easy for us to feel apathetic and indifferent toward noncritical patients. The less free time we have, the more demands on our schedules, and the more pressured we feel by nonclinical obligations the more pronounced this apathy becomes.

Unfortunately, one night, I lost my temper after a woman called, distraught, at two AM because she ran out of a compounded prescription for progesterone yam cream that she was using to treat her nuanced hormone imbalance. I had just returned home and crawled into bed after thirty-six hours of nonstop clinical work that included an emergency cesarean section and several other challenging surgical cases. The woman on the phone was clearly distressed from her lack of compounded yams; however, I felt annoyed and indignant. How could this woman be calling in the middle of the night about irrelevant cream when I had just ignored even my most basic biological needs to operate emergently and handle a number of critically ill patients? A family had almost lost their baby, and I had been working for thirty-six hours. Was she seriously calling about an "emergency" cream?

My indignation about my perceived greater suffering from working long hours and handling medical emergencies colored my ability to speak rationally to this patient. I felt angry at her for disturbing me after what I had just been through, and I could not empathize with her situation at all. We both hung up in frustration and went on to tell our stories later, me of the seemingly ridiculous patient, and her of the rude and uncaring physician.

In all we have seen and in all that we do, it becomes automatic to see the world backward through the lens of the worst we have experienced, comparing it to the situation at hand. Patients, however, see the world forward, through the lens of how awful they feel at any given moment, with a frame of reference that does not include the death and destruction that is commonplace for us. A patient's mildest symptom may be cause for legitimate concern, yet from our relative view, many complaints are unfounded. Repeating this dynamic day after day can lead to anger at the patients for stealing our time with noncritical concerns, and to apathy toward their well-being when they present with seemingly insignificant problems. We plod through our days feeling as if we are wasting our time on ridiculousness and then getting stuck with the task of required documentation. The relentless parade of these patients makes our contribution feel meaningless, and our days fill with frustration and apathy.

We are also often plagued by feelings of futility, treating patients who come to our offices and emergency departments with conditions related entirely to their personal lifestyle choices. Much of the hypertension, diabetes, obesity, lung disease, and heart disease we find in front of us could be altered through lifestyle changes, yet patients often expect prescriptive solutions. Similarly, we see tragic accidents following too much to drink, horrific injuries from child abuse, addicts manipulating the system for drugs, demented patients simply dropped off in our hospitals because no one wants to deal with them anymore, and a seemingly endless parade of patients to whom we have nothing useful to offer. The medical care we can provide feels futile, and as the parade keeps rolling, we become more depressed, more cynical, and more indifferent.

Eventually, we may no longer genuinely feel for anyone who presents for our care, and we may begin to view patients as thieves of our time instead of distressed clients in search of compassion. The rare experience of taking care of a suffering patient with a critical problem who follows through with our advice and improves to live a better life is not nearly enough to balance the hundreds of other relatively disappointing cases. The natural default emotion is disappointment, then indifference, yielding depersonalization toward patients and then, eventually, everyone else. Unfortunately, what we have trained ourselves to manage at work spills over into our personal lives, and soon, we feel next to nothing when our spouse is upset, our child is crying, or a friend is relating an emotional story.

Shaun says, "The evening I truly became aware of this phenomenon, I found myself having to really stop and pay attention to the slighted feelings my daughter had after a frustrating day in middle school. After my day of unbelievable sadness at work, the seemingly simple problem my daughter was facing seemed annoying, and I felt almost irritated at being dragged into it. Reflecting, I'm sad that I trivialized her pain based on comparison to the pain of my patients. Thankfully, we had a good conversation, with me apologizing and her expressing understanding, before we brainstormed solutions to her situation together."

At the peak of my burnout experience, I'm horrified to report, I cruelly brushed off a friend when he called me midday to tell me his father had a recurrence of cancer. Instead of feeling natural empathy with his distress, I inexplicably felt interrupted and almost annoyed that he had called. Although I was in full-on survival mode at the time, I couldn't possibly have behaved any worse. He very graciously later accepted my sincere apology, but the damage to our friendship was palpable for months, and I have never forgiven myself for that disastrous and hurtful conversation. Typing this, I cringe now as I recall it.

These examples may seem extreme, but ask yourself truthfully how many times you simply tune out your children, spouse, or friends. Eventually, with perpetual desensitization, many of us stop trying to listen and simply stumble along just as numbly in our intimate relationships as we do at the office. With our professional insight, we see what we're doing but can't find the switch to turn the numbness off. We then berate ourselves for working so hard to become physicians who aren't truly helping many patients and whose training has seemingly morphed us into cruel and insensitive zombies.

At times, we feel surrounded by relative ridiculousness and feel that our contributions are an absolute sham. To further compensate, we often reach for extremes or medicate ourselves to manage the pain of our over-whelming disappointment. We become junkies, seeking out the next adrenaline rush by achieving the next seemingly impossible goal or rely-ing on substances or social media to handle our lives.

One thing is clear: Everyone suffers. Whether your crisis is lack of clean water, unmanageable debt, feelings of not being loved, a strained mar-riage, a diagnosis of cancer, existentialism, a late-night hormone imbal-ance, or physician burnout, the suffering is authentic and impossible to stratify when felt from inside.

Our jobs as physicians and also as humans are therefore not to sort out who is suffering more than whom, or who deserves our time and atten-tion. Our task is to offer our kindness, care, and attention to whoever appears and then allow that individual to do what he or she will going forward. Neither our compassion nor our kindness is to be rationed for extreme or deserving cases; it is to be offered universally, understanding that to be human is to experience suffering and to offer compassion is to soothe humanity. As providers, we're not treating degrees of illness or degrees of suffering but rather the human condition in all its permuta-tions, whether it appears as obesity, anxiety, hemorrhage, malaria, a tear-ful child, an angry spouse, or road rage. Most importantly, *we ourselves are to be included in our own compassion.*

What began as self-preservation has morphed into self-destructive behavior, and conditioning ourselves not to feel has ultimately eliminated the joy from our personal and professional lives.

Shaun and I thus propose that the depersonalization of the modern burnout epidemic is not something that occurs irrationally. As physicians, we have specifically trained ourselves into this state so we can professionally care for our patients and avoid feeling what would be overwhelming and inappropriate emotion on the job. In doing so, we have numbed ourselves so exceedingly well that we can neither connect genuinely with our loved ones nor find compassion for ourselves. What began as self-preservation has morphed into self-destructive behavior, and conditioning ourselves not to feel has ultimately eliminated the joy from our personal and professional lives. Reviving emotion—and thereby joy—requires ditching the substances, attending to ourselves, and reframing our outlook toward others in the context of our shared humanity.

What you can do to revive your situation:

1. Make a list of all the ways you numb yourself, and evaluate whether these are helping you experience peace and ease in your life or are hindering you.

2. Identify people and relationships that have suffered because you have become apathetic or because you are so skilled at suppressing your emotions.

3. Look genuinely into your relationships to see whose feelings or which situation you may have trivialized by comparing it to your workplace experience. Apologize to the affected person or people if it feels appropriate, no matter how much time has passed since the incident you noted.

4. Feeling complex emotions is impossible at first, so find your way back to your emotional self by starting with physical sensations. Start by asking yourself what you feel physically, such as your heart pounding, your leg shaking, your eye twitching, hunger, headache, and the like. This will give you confidence to realize that you actually can and do feel something. Move gradually from physical sensations to emotions.

5. Get a coach or mentor to help you through this process, especially if you have damaged or distant interpersonal relationships as a result of extreme numbing behavior or suppressed emotion. (I found an eight-week Mindful Self-Compassion™ class to be helpful, and Shaun worked successfully with Jamie Beeson in her CHANGE program.)

6. Following a tragic or stressful medical case, surgery, or litigation process, intentionally debrief with someone who genuinely understands what you went through. Typically, this will

have to be a trusted colleague or someone who truly understands the medical profession; however, processing your experience with a counselor or pastor can still be extremely beneficial. It should not feel routine, for example, to formally pronounce a patient dead one minute, return to doing office wellness exams the next, then pick a few things up from Target on your way home, watch television, go to bed, then arrive at work the next day as if nothing unusual has happened.

What organizations can do to support providers and improve engagement:

1. Encourage providers to attend Mindful Self-Compassion™ or similar courses to stay in touch with their emotions and improve their interpersonal relationships. Cover the registration fees for these courses.

2. Encourage formal debriefing processes following traumas, emergencies, and deaths, or even at the end of each workweek. We're so busy that we typically bulldoze through traumatic patient-care experiences and move on with our days. Having a formal processes to unpack these emotions can help us learn to stop "stuffing it" until we erupt uncontrollably. Involve your physicians in developing the debriefing processes you envision implementing.

3. Create a resource list of physicians who have been through legal proceedings who can emotionally support other doctors going through lawsuits, and make that support readily available.

4. Build relief into schedules, such that if a provider has an extremely stressful or taxing experience, he or she has a way to arrange immediate time off to regroup without risk of punitive action. For example, our office uses a float doctor who sees add-on patients and covers clinic when others are called away, out for illness, or taking time off.

7.

THE "NEXT LOGICAL STEP" SYNDROME

If you do not change direction, you may end up where you are heading.

—Lau Tzu

ave you ever stopped for a moment to consider how you became a doctor, a spouse, or a parent? Where did your mortgage or your PhD come from, exactly? If you are anything like us, chances are, you arrived where you currently are in life by simply following the next logical step. Certainly, something powerful compelled you to persevere through the rigors of medical education and residency, and of course, you likely chose your professional field and your spouse. But at any point in the game, did you sit down and truly consider whether you actually wanted a spouse, child, career, dog, or mortgage?

We're guessing you began medical school and then followed the yellow brick road through the perils of passing exams, attending clerkships, applying for residency, completing training, securing employment, getting board certified, paying down student debt, contributing to a 401(k), and so on. Maybe somewhere along the way, you fell in love and got married, bought a car, bought a house, had 2.5 kids, got a dog, bought a bigger car, bought a bigger house, took on a better job, and settled in for the long haul. As dissatisfaction started nibbling at you in the workplace, maybe you looked around at your life, family, and financial situation and wondered, *How did I get here?* Maybe thereafter you had a midlife crisis, got divorced, had an affair, bought a motorcycle, or simply resigned yourself to your chosen path. Or maybe you discovered that you absolutely love your path and celebrated your good fortune with a party or family vacation.

Unfortunately, many of the healthcare professionals we have met suffer from what we have coined the "next logical step" syndrome. Symptoms include fatigue, indifference, rage, irritability, anxiety, and an overwhelming desire to sell everything you own and live anonymously in a trailer by the river or a hut in Costa Rica. You will recognize this insidious condition when, one day, you awake to realize that you no longer love your job, you feel emotionally distant from your spouse, you secretly wish to re-home your children (at least sometimes), your finances are a mess, and there is no relief in sight from these overwhelming responsibilities other than putting your head down and heavyheartedly stumbling forward.

To cure this condition, you must first acknowledge that you got where you are by blindly following the next logical step instead of deliberating choosing in congruence with your values. Next, you must reconsider every aspect of your life and make a conscious choice to embrace what you have or to move toward an alternative.

Rest assured, you are locked in to exactly *nothing* in your life. Every single component is up for consideration, including your marriage, employment, health, fitness, daily schedule, savings plan, friendships, and residence—*everything*. Of course when it comes to certain subjects, such as taking care of your children or remaining married, you likely feel a moral or personal obligation to stay the course; in that case, you have actually chosen to honor that moral compass and continue on, but you are absolutely not trapped.

We're purposefully using an extreme example here, but you could, in fact, choose to quit your job tomorrow. You likely wouldn't, but you technically could. You could absolutely choose to not go to work anymore or pay your bills, though you would then be choosing the consequences of not working or of bankruptcy. This may sound absolutely ridiculous, but feeling compelled to behave in certain ways because of societal norms, guilt, or your personal moral compass is an entirely different situation than being forced or trapped into doing anything. The truth is, we choose our behavior every day, all day, and recognizing that you don't have to continue miserably drifting along on autopilot and can literally re-choose (or not) every aspect of your life, item by item, with its associated consequences can feel empowering.

You don't have to wait until you irreparably crack before making some decisions about the course of your life or career.

Correcting my course required getting a divorce, temporarily re-homing a pet, taking six months of unpaid leave from my job, selling my furniture, renting out my home, going to massage school, and living for several months in a third-world country. For Shaun, joining forces with a global maternal-health project, redistributing some unsatisfying professional responsibilities, and rearranging her patient-care schedule did the trick. Some may consider this thought process a midlife crisis, and to be fair, re-choosing what you already have versus some alternative that seems extreme often begins with a crisis—but you don't have to wait until you irreparably crack before making some decisions about the course of your life or career. Do it now! Get pen and paper and ask yourself some questions:

> Do I choose to stay married, separate, or get a divorce? What does each of those situations actually look like for me?

> Do I keep my pets and my responsibility to care for them, or do I find them new homes?

> Do I stay with my current employer and keep my schedule, do I make modifications, or do I look for a new source of income?

Do I complete my tenure as chair of this important committee, or do I resign?

Do I live in my current house, or do I move to an apartment, a different town, or a new country?

Do I stay in medicine or become a dog groomer?

Okay, we're being a bit ridiculous, but you get the idea. Though we're in no way suggesting that the solution to physician burnout is to abandon your pets or family, we are suggesting that you take a serious look at the entirety of your current situation with fresh eyes. Leave no stone unturned; think it through and deliberately choose every single aspect of your life over again, or an alternative. Instead of miserably drifting along on autopilot, you will discover that there are opportunities everywhere to either correct your alignment or to embrace the status quo. As you do so, you free yourself from the bondage created by the "next logical step" syndrome that got you into this mess and create the space to enjoy the life *you* have chosen.

If upending your life seems extreme, consider this: Instead of taking the next *logical* step, try taking the next best step. As discussed in chapter 1, identify the basic parameters of your ideal life and begin by taking the next best step in that direction.

What you can do to revive your situation:

1.   What "logical" steps did you take to get where you are?

2.   Did you follow the yellow brick road, or did you get where you are with deliberate intention?

3.   Can you recall a moment when you thought you might be off track yet continued forward anyway?

4.   Choose every aspect of your life again, or choose an alternative, then wholeheartedly embrace what you have chosen, without reservation. For example, if you choose to remain in your current intimate relationship or to stay in medicine, then do whatever it takes to find joy, peace, and ease in that situation, realizing that you have fully claimed that decision. Or if you realize that you are in medicine, live in San Diego, or bought a mega-mansion by default, not intention, plot a new course immediately and fully embrace the challenges revealed by that decision.

5.   If upending your life seems extreme, consider this: Instead of taking the next *logical* step, try taking the next best step. As discussed in chapter 1, identify the basic parameters of your ideal life and begin by taking the next best step in that direction.

8.

THE HYPOCRITIC OATH

We don't have to engage in grand, heroic actions to participate in the process of change. Small acts, when multiplied by millions of people, can transform the world.

—Howard Zinn

"Oh my God, I can't even look at you!" exclaimed the patient when I walked in the room. She had been transferred to the hospital for cesarean section after attempting an unsuccessful out-of-hospital birth, and I had just entered to meet her. On my nose was a splint flanked by two huge black eyes following an operation I'd had four days prior. I looked more like a panda than a physician, and of course I was working twenty-four hours on call, having never given a thought to the fact that it may not be reasonable or appropriate to return to full-time employment less than a week after surgery. Truthfully, I felt guilty for taking off more than the weekend to recover. Shaun once fell acutely ill with appendicitis on Saturday, had surgery later that day, and returned to full-time work on Tuesday. Honestly, what were we thinking?

As surgeons, we would never advise our patients to behave in this manner. In fact, we would likely label them noncompliant for blatantly disregarding our advice to take time off work postoperatively and return only when medically cleared. Of course, neither Shaun nor I returned for a postoperative check. Why would we? We thought we were fine.

> **It's as if we are stuck in some sick competition of one-upmanship to see who can stay awake the longest, work the most hours, see the most patients, miss the most family outings, or persevere through the most serious illness. ***

This superhuman charade may seem valiant at first, but eventually, it just becomes stupid. Who do we think we are, staying up all night, skipping meals, working twenty-four or more hours in a row on call? Why do we resist implementing work-hour restrictions or scoff at those who cannot "pull their weight"? Why do we think we can get away with having coffee for breakfast, peanut butter from the patient food drawer for lunch, and stale doughnuts from the nurses' lounge overnight? Who among us doesn't know a colleague (or maybe ourselves) who has crashed their vehicle while driving critically impaired with fatigue? Who gave us permission to skip pap smears, postpone mammograms, evade counseling, and not even bother with health-maintenance exams? Why do we come to work sneezing, hacking, vomiting, and febrile? Why do we so sternly advise patients on how to care for themselves yet assume those same instructions don't apply when we look in the mirror? It's as if we are stuck in some sick competition of one-upmanship to see who can stay awake the longest, work the most hours, see the most patients, miss the most family outings, or persevere through the most serious illness.

We legitimize our behavior, feeling we are justified in sacrificing our own well-being because we're doing so in service to others, but does this really make sense?

Hmmm, I wonder why we feel so crappy? Maybe it's because we haven't had a decent night of sleep in years? Maybe it's our deplorable nutritional habits, our complete disregard for our own sound medical advice, or the relentless way we push ourselves to the brink of exhaustion day after day, year after year? No, scrap that; it's obviously just the unreasonable demands of the medical industrial complex, the complexities of the EMR, or the frustrations of documentation.

Get serious! This is an unbelievably critical problem. We legitimize our behavior, feeling we are justified in sacrificing our own well-being because we're doing so in service to others, but does this really make sense? Is it realistically sustainable? You know how you feel, and we're guessing that if you're reading this book it's not good at times. It's no secret that chronic stress negatively affects our physiology, interferes with our neurotransmitters, and increases our risk of diabetes, heart disease, and numerous other conditions. As scientists, we know the impact of stress on our physical selves, and as individuals, we can feel this stress literally chipping away at us.

If we are to be authentic healthcare providers in the twenty-first century, navigating the challenges all around us, we simply have to take better care of ourselves. Not only are we dropping like flies from suicide, burnout, and exhaustion, but fewer individuals are entering clinical medicine, and those who complete training are retiring earlier each year. In an effort to maintain our survival as a profession and our roles as models for patients, we can no longer behave like unruly teenagers. We're not Spartans; we're doctors—and it would behoove us to, at the very least, start modeling the behavior we expect from our patients.

Do you feel Mrs. Jones should eat less sugar and consume more fiber to control her diabetes? Doctor, what's in your lunchbox? Did you advise Ms. Smith that her depression is worsened in part because she is overextended, overworked, overstressed, and isn't getting enough rest? Doctor, have you looked at your lifestyle? Did you tell Mr. Scott to try yoga and get physical therapy for his low back pain? Doctor, how's your lumbago? Did you advise Mr. Davis that his mood might improve if he spent less time in front of the TV and more time outside? Doctor, have you checked your own screen-sky ratio? Did you gently suggest to Ms. Adams this morning that she cut down her wine consumption? Doctor, what's in your glass?

It seems that despite our years of scientific study, we have forgotten the very basics of well-being and assign blame everywhere but our own disastrous lifestyles.

What if, starting today, we discard the "hypocritic" oath we mistakenly took—and simply take better care of ourselves? Shaun and I guess that we would not only feel better immediately but also, in the space we free up, might find creative solutions to larger issues. The so-called burnout epidemic has no chance of improving until we stop burning the candle at both ends and slow down. At this point, we are all so rushed and exhausted that we don't even have time to do any of the introspective exercises in this book or contemplate workable solutions to our personal and professional crises. If we expect to be taken seriously as we petition for system improvements, we must start with our personal inventory. What steps can you take, effective immediately, to drop your superhuman charade and address your well-being?

Strategies Melissa implemented:

1. Actually had a pap, a mammogram, an eye exam, a skin check, and laboratory studies, which led to new glasses and fewer headaches.

2. More often than not, limited consecutive work hours on call to twenty-four.

3. Stopped filling the post-call day with clinic and chores, instead designating it solely for rest and recovery.

4. Started clinic on some days around noon, spending the morning walking the dog, hiking, or trail running.

5. Ended some clinic days at four PM to have time to prepare a nutritious dinner to share with family.

6. Booked monthly relaxation massages.

7. Developed a spiritual practice.

Strategies Shaun implemented:

1. Worked with her partners to come up with a call and surgery schedule that didn't leave her (and her staff) feeling run ragged.

2. Clarified patient schedule preferences for on-call and post-call days to make sure she could take care of patients well.

3. Looked ahead and arranged the schedule to accommodate children's sporting and musical events, which was important to her and her family.

4. Planned monthly date nights with her husband (which was a huge improvement over the annual date nights from years past).

5. Exercised four days a week with no time mandate. (She used to think if it wasn't an hour, it didn't count.)

6. Made time to read personal-development books.

7. Cultivated relationships with family and friends, which had long been neglected.

8. Changed habits around sleep time so she could feel well rested!

What you can do to revive your situation:

1. List where you have shortchanged yourself in terms of your health and well-being.

2. Give yourself permission to attend to your basic needs, such as eating nutritious food, getting restful sleep, having time with family, and exercising without guilt or apology.

Give yourself permission to attend to your basic needs

---

3. Evaluate how much of your perceived lack of time to care for yourself is self-inflicted. Is it really true that you don't have time, or have you filled your time with other priorities? For example, do you really have to see patients or operate on part or all of your post-call day? What would the true consequences be if you reduced your patient load on these days? Do you truly have to work six twelve-hour shifts in a week? What would three shifts look like? What would an eight-hour shift look like instead?

Is it really true that you don't have time, or have you filled your time with other priorities?

---

4. Don't ridicule or disrespect colleagues who have prioritized work-life balance or altered the way they practice medicine to accommodate well-being as a priority.

What organizations can do to support providers and improve engagement:

1. Support providers who request to work a decreased schedule after twenty-four-hour call or similar shift. This is a patient-safety issue. Would you want someone to make critical decisions about your medical care or operate on you after they have already been awake and working for twenty-four or more hours in a row? Would you even allow them to give you a ride home in this condition?

2. Provide inviting, comfortable, and relaxing sleep rooms with clean showers for providers who work long shifts. A hot shower and a three-hour nap can mean the difference between a disgruntled provider and a provider who can function reasonably well the subsequent day. Having a nice resting space for physicians shows that you notice and appreciate the fact that they are working all night and into the next day.

3. Have a small fitness space available in your facility where providers who are working on weekends or covering lengthy shifts can take an exercise break.

4. Make arrangements to have nutritious food options and decent coffee available twenty-four hours a day for providers who work off hours. Nothing is worse than trying to do an operation late at night when the only food available pre-op is from vending machines or the nurses' station.

5. Create a well-being committee dedicated to supporting the needs of providers, and then make every effort to actually implement the committee's recommendations in a meaningful way.

6.   Incentivize physicians and other staff to take excellent care of their health, with rewards for cycling to work or discounts on insurance for not smoking, for maintaining normal weight, or for achieving optimal lab values.

7.   Proactively look for ways to use your organization and its employees to model healthy behaviors in the communities it serves.

8.   Allow providers such as Emergency Department physicians, anesthesiologists, and hospitalists to split or share their "traditional" eight-, twelve-, or twenty-four-hour shifts if they request to do so.

9.

PERCEIVED LIMITATIONS

The key is not to prioritize what's on your schedule,
but to schedule your priorities.

—Stephen Covey

Perceived limitations are just that: perceptions, paper tigers, issues that aren't real except in your mind. These rascals are everywhere, shutting down creativity and trapping clinicians right and left. I first encountered these ubiquitous troublemakers during my time as a weight-loss coach when, for example, my clients were absolutely fixed on what constituted breakfast, lunch, and dinner. In their minds, it was cereal, bagels, or oatmeal for breakfast, sandwiches or burgers for lunch, and a hearty meat-starch-salad combo with dessert for dinner. Salad for breakfast? No way. Six nectarines for lunch? Impossible. Raw vegetables for dinner? Never going to happen. Skip dessert? Now that's just crazy talk! It was not because these foods were utterly unacceptable options for caloric or nutrient intake that my clients didn't want to consider them, but rather that my proposed sustenance didn't match the ideas these clients had in their minds about what to eat. The truth is, any food can be eaten at any time of day, and the *perception* as to what constitutes an acceptable meal was the actual obstacle to making a relevant change.

So, what is one of the biggest paper tigers of clinical practice? Scheduling—otherwise known as work martyrdom. We admit, the paralysis that comes from perceived necessary patient-care schedules had us chained to the office at one point too, but we cracked the code! Here's the secret: When you see patients, for how many hours a day, and on what days, is entirely your prerogative. You can start your day at ten AM and end at two PM or seven PM. You can take a three-hour break midday. You can start at seven AM and work five days a week, or only two days. You can split your on-call, hospitalist, or Emergency Department shift with other providers.

We're not suggesting that these changes would be without consequence; we're merely proposing that an alternate schedule is possible.

"No I can't!" you're screaming at this page right now. "You don't know my office manager, my situation, my contract, or my partners!" you rant. "Those are idiotic suggestions!" We're not suggesting that these changes would be without consequence; we're merely proposing that an alternate schedule is possible.

Before you throw this book in the trash, think for a moment: What and who are actually controlling your schedule? An honest look may reveal some of the following:

1. You feel obligated to see the same number of patients as your partners and "pull your weight."

2. You feel obligated to see every patient who calls and requests an appointment, especially if it is an established patient, a referral from a colleague, or your neighbor's mother.

3. Your office is open from eight AM to five PM daily and those are the hours you feel expected to work.

4. Everyone else works twenty-four-hour call shifts, so you believe you should too.

5. You have historically started clinic at eight AM and have never considered starting at ten AM or one PM.

6. The way your contract is written, you are expected to work certain hours, and this arrangement is nonnegotiable.

7. Your institution has made it clear that you are to see more patients this year than last year.

8. Your existing patients have trouble scheduling appointments because you have no openings for months.

9. You are solely and personally responsible for your existing patients, and no one could care for them as well as you, or that you are obligated not to "dump" the care of these patients onto someone else.

10. You have to generate a certain number of work RVUs to earn your current salary.

We would like to propose that all of the above may be absolutely true; however, none of them unequivocally preclude you from setting a different schedule for yourself immediately. In the same way my weight-loss clients' minds refused to consider salad for breakfast or nectarines for lunch, your mind is simply telling you it's not possible to have control over your schedule.

> **Your moral obligation is to provide excellent care to those patients you can accommodate in a way that does not ruin your own family, health, or life. It is not your personal responsibility to single-handedly martyr yourself to accommodate the physician shortage in America by working yourself to personal ruin.**

"But what about my moral responsibility to care for patients, to pull my weight with my partners, to uphold the standards set by my profession?" you might ask. Although you may desperately desire to live up to every perceived expectation set by society, your hospital, and the clinicians around you, or you even feel obligated to work more than others around you in the name of workplace martyrdom, we propose an alternative. If, for example, you are a cardiologist, it is in no way your personal responsibility to see every referral, or every patient with a heart condition in your community. Your moral obligation is to provide excellent care to those patients you can accommodate in a way that does not ruin your own family, health, or life. It is not your personal responsibility to single-handedly martyr yourself to accommodate the physician shortage in America by working yourself to personal ruin. Your longevity in medicine hinges on your ability to provide compassionate care in a sustainable manner, and every provider's threshold for excellence varies. This can be especially challenging for solo providers in rural areas or for busy specialists, who literally have no one else available to attend to a patient they turn away. Our design and our training compel us to care for all comers, and many providers do so at significant personal and professional cost.

One of the most heart-wrenching stories we have encountered on this topic is that of a young specialist physician who tearfully explained that he had never eaten a weekday dinner with his five-year-old child or tucked her into bed. He worked all day at the office, then stayed late to complete documentation and review charts for the next day. We spoke with him as he was seeking help in becoming more efficient in clinic so he could care for his perpetually increasing patient load more expeditiously. He envisioned working faster as the only solution to freeing up evenings to spend with his family. His motivation was true, and no other similar specialists were readily available to care for all the patients who called for appointments, yet the cost of his dedication to work was also clearly apparent.

When we proposed that he instead end clinic at three PM, the idea was met with stern resistance. "I have a long wait list of critical patients; my office manager is already upset about patient access to appointments; I'm obligated to see these referrals; my colleagues see patients until five PM; and my work RVUs will be down," came the litany of excuses. All were paper tigers; nothing solid was truly stopping him from going to his manager the very next day and stating, effective immediately, that his last patient appointment needed to be booked at three PM so he could share evenings with his family.

Would there be consequences? Absolutely. Some patients would have to seek care out of town and might be unhappy, thereby compromising his patient-satisfaction scores. He might have to adjust his employment status and benefits to 0.8 or 0.5 instead of 1.0, or decrease his work RVU target, or come to terms with the fact that other specialists work more hours than he does, or, in the worst-case scenario, risk being fired and have to find a new part-time position that accommodates family time. He might also have to come to terms with the guilt he may feel from no longer prioritizing patient care above family; however, his mandatory enslavement to the current schedule was absolutely imaginary.

Once I took control of my schedule, I adjusted it frequently over the years depending on my life circumstance, and I've been fortunate to work for progressive employers and with flexible partners who have supported me in doing so. One year, I trained for an Ironman triathlon and used my commute to prepare. I jogged nine miles to work and then nine miles home two days a week. On those days, I scheduled patients from ten AM to three PM. I also took an entire day off to meet with a coach and to cycle outdoors with my training partner. Naturally, I generated fewer work RVUs and earned less money during that season and, importantly, I recruited support from my physician partners prior to making clinic adjustments. I also finished an Ironman, and I don't regret modifying my schedule or asking my partners for support to do so.

To be clear, we're *not* suggesting that you adjust your clinic to accommodate every nuance of your life, or that you eat salad for breakfast or jog to work; however, we do recommend that you go back to chapter 1 and look at your values assessment. If taking excellent care of yourself is high on the list, then that warrants specifically altering your work schedule to prioritize nutrition and exercise, even if that choice seems nonsensical to those in your immediate microcosm. If spending time with family or being outside is high on your values list, arrange family and nature time first, then fill in your clinic around it. Taking this approach doesn't mean you don't care anymore about patients; it just means you don't care disproportionately more about work than about the other components of life.

It is *equally* commendable to be a physician who joyfully cares for large volumes of patients at all hours as it is to be one who contributes on a different scale.

Alternatively, if your values assessment ranks being universally available for patient care or being the highest financial producer in your office near the top, then honor that carefully. It is *equally* commendable to be a physician who joyfully cares for large volumes of patients at all hours as it is to be one who contributes on a different scale. The important thing is to adjust your medical contribution to best align with *your life as a whole*, not to simply work excessively out of guilt, comparison, habit, or compulsion.

Ultimately, we are all responsible for the hours we work, and we all chose our schedules wholeheartedly. By this we mean that we selected our medical specialties, our places of employment, and our full- or part-time positions. Each of us negotiated our hours, our salaries, and the terms of our contracts without coercion by violent enforcers. With physician shortages abounding, all of us could change our situations entirely and rapidly if we chose to do so. We could take locum tenens assignments and work one week a month, but most of us don't. Maybe we agreed to our hours to earn a certain salary, live in a specific area, or maintain important relationships, or maybe some of us work the hours we do out of guilt or peer pressure, or to prove that we are as tough as the next guy. Whatever the reason, lamenting the number of hours we spend on the job neglects our role in creating the schedule we currently enjoy, and disempowers us from making alterations that both honor the integrity of our profession and respect our individual well-being.

Are you worried how your decision to build your schedule will impose on your colleagues or office staff? Have you considered including them in the discussion about work hours or convening as an office team to assess the best way to improve scheduling and access for everyone? Each person's values assessment varies, and the comprehensive schedule can reflect that accordingly. Some providers actually prefer to work longer hours or take night call, while others are happy part-time. In our office, specifically, a team meeting about schedules led to greater patient access while simultaneously ensuring that none of us ever again had to operate post-call.

After all, are we really providing excellent care when we treat patients while we're feeling resentful or when we operate after working all night?

The goal of this chapter is not to try to encourage doctors to weasel out of clinic or to shift the burden of patient care to others but to find a schedule that is reasonable, manageable, and in line with your personal values. After all, are we really providing excellent care when we treat patients while we're feeling resentful or when we operate after working all night? How many of us have even actually looked into the possibility of restructuring our hours at the office or our shiftwork on call? We're guessing not many at all.

If you're happy with your setup as-is, or if you truly value yourself by the hours you work, by all means continue, or even expand! If, however, you feel imprisoned by your schedule, with no hope of parole, then ask your-self if you can at least *try* to make a change. As we have already reviewed, time spent either in or out of alignment with what is important to you greatly influences your personal and professional experience, and your enjoyment of medicine depends on it.

What you can do to revive your situation:

1. Honestly evaluate your schedule and make changes accordingly.

2. Ask yourself what is truly stopping you from starting your day an hour later or ending an hour sooner. What is truly stopping you from working an extended shift one day and a shorter one the next to accommodate your full-time position? (For example, I once negotiated an arrangement in which I saw patients from eight AM to seven PM on Tuesdays in exchange for additional free time later in the week.) What is truly stopping you from taking your post-call day off or ending it earlier? Is it the requirements of your organization or the expectation of your partners? Do you want to make a change? If so, what are you willing to sacrifice for this change? Would you give up your nurse, accept a lower salary and reduced benefits, or move out of your office? Would you risk losing your position entirely and be faced with finding new employment?

3. Find out from your manager or employer what the actual consequences would be for you to restructure your hours in a way that aligns with your values.

4. Who will take care of your patients? If you work in a group, collectively brainstorm how to structure scheduling for everyone such that the best care can be provided to the most patients without destroying providers. Collaboration and creativity are infinitely more effective than judging each other for number of hours worked or not worked and comparing your work habits with those of others.

5. If you are one of only a few providers in a rural area, ask specifically for regularly scheduled outside coverage to give you a break. This request is completely reasonable and appropriate. Having worked as a solo provider in a rural town myself, I now love going into these areas periodically as a locum tenens provider to offer relief to the community physician.

6. Refuse to spend your weekends, evenings, and vacation time on documentation. Build time for charting into your daily schedule, even if it means seeing one or two fewer patients per day. Alternatively, protect a dedicated half day per week for documentation, even if it means a reduced clinic schedule. We know a number of providers who have budgeted specific charting time into their days, with excellent quality of life improvements.

7. Each week, look at the schedule for the subsequent week and find overbookings, gaps that could be filled with acute patients, and other conflicts in advance so you are not blindsided on any given day by schedule disasters.

What organizations can do to support providers and improve engagement:

1. *Don't panic after reading this chapter!* We know not all providers can work haphazardly, modifying their schedules to suit their preferences. Not every physician will. In fact, the inherent workaholic and responsible natures of many physicians will preclude them from making any changes whatsoever. There can, however, be a built-in level of flexibility that allows for some scheduling autonomy. This will improve the overall quality of care provided, and the ultimate longevity of physicians in your organization.

2. Consider designating providers as full time or 0.8 or 0.5 FTEs and associating a specific patient-contact-hour requirement with that designation. Then allow providers to set their schedules accordingly so they meet their requirements. This arrangement feels more accommodating than mandating that your providers see patients from eight AM to five PM four days a week on your terms. Alternatively, if you require providers to work on your schedule, be clear with them about that during the hiring process so they know exactly what they are agreeing to do when they sign a contract.

3. Support high producers with the resources they need to work smoothly and efficiently. If you are lucky enough to have physicians who are physically and emotionally dedicated to working extended hours, go out of your way to support them. This degree of effort is the exception, not the norm, as patient care can be relentless and taxing. Many of us who presently work reduced hours felt compelled to do so because the personal cost of our workload outweighed the benefits of our contribution. Supporting the logistics and staffing needs of

those providers who are high performers will show your appreciation and also lengthen the years they are able to work at a high level of intensity.

Many of us who presently work reduced hours felt compelled to do so because the personal cost of our workload outweighed the benefits of our contribution.

---

4. Ask all your providers what their ideal practice would look like, and offer to help them achieve it or, at the very least, to incorporate some components of their vision into their current environment.

5. Ask your providers individually what type of support they feel would benefit them, make them more efficient, best utilize their skills, and improve their experience at work; then take tangible actions to help them implement what they described. Even asking the question of them shows them that provider well-being is on your radar and that you genuinely care to address it.

6. Be extremely clear about expectations for hours worked, number of patients seen, and levels of production when hiring physicians and revisit these often with your existing staff. Also describe in plain language how a provider would realistically make schedule changes and streamline the process to do so. Having a clear understanding of corporate expectations and the processes to make changes helps providers work effectively within their organizations.

10.

MONEY MADNESS

Success is getting what you want. Happiness is wanting what you get.

—Dale Carnegie

Millions of dollars slip through our gifted hands year after year. Yes, we have student loans and kids and mortgages, but let's face it: while we may be genius practitioners, many of us are absolutely terrible money managers. When I first found myself in the midst of a burnout crisis, I desperately wanted to quit medical practice. I was ready to quit; I had reached my breaking point—but alas, I had no money. What? Where did it go? Hadn't I earned several hundred thousand dollars a year for the past decade? Wasn't I wealthy? I'd been working day and night saving lives, not flipping burgers; surely I had plenty of cash in the bank, in a mattress, in an offshore account? Nope, not true! I was absolutely trapped by my own money madness, the same affliction felt by wage earners nationwide who spend too much and save too little with no viable escape plan.

At first I lamented my plight, blaming every possible outside force for my lack of funds, including taxes, student loans, and my costly divorce. Then I looked around my house and saw an unused sauna, a hot tub, clothing with the tags still on, rotting food in the fridge, barely used ski equipment, a $1500 road bike, high-end dog food, a housekeeper, hair dye, a lawn service, and my gym membership (complete with personal trainer).

The fact of the matter was that even though I had done well in some areas, such as eliminating student loans, paying off credit cards monthly, funding my IRA, and securing an emergency cash fund, my spending was

unthoughtful, my budget nonexistent, and my savings abysmal compared to my earnings. I was somehow still living paycheck to paycheck
even with a six-figure income. Had I played my cards more consciously,
I could have easily had over a million dollars saved before turning forty.
Then, when I was faced with professional crisis, money wouldn't have
been such an obstacle.

Fortunately, being a single person with no children and a bit of a wild
streak, I solved my financial woes almost immediately and was able to
recalibrate my career with a six month sabbatical and $60,000 cash in
hand. My solution included renting out my house and temporarily moving in with friends. I found a lovely short-term home for my dog and vis-
ited her daily (truthfully, she loved hanging out with canine friends all
day more than sitting alone at my house). I sold everything I deemed
excessive, including the sauna, the hot tub, my sports equipment, some
artwork, the furniture, my designer sunglasses, my jewelry, and my tread-
mill. I canceled my gym membership and every auto-ship program send-
ing monthly installments of protein shakes, celebrity shampoo, and
anti-wrinkle cream. When I rented out my house, all special services,
including housekeeping, lawn care, and utilities, became the tenant's
responsibility.

These changes funded my time off and paved the way for a future free
from financial bondage. Recalibrating my expenses led me to the peace
and ease of an extremely simple lifestyle and a very low cost of living. My
basic annual expenses thereafter, including housing, pet care, trans-
portation, and insurance, dropped to under $40,000, and the pressure I
felt to earn this amount of income became minimal. A few locums
assignments would easily cover this cost, as would innumerable other
sources of income outside of medical practice. If I wanted to walk away
from medicine tomorrow, I could, but the fact that I no longer have the
pressure to meet the production required for my prior salary has lifted so
much weight from my shoulders that I have continued to work. Without

the financial noose around my neck, I have found medical practice unbelievably more enjoyable. Streamlining my financial situation has been the single biggest contributor to my well-being and professional satisfaction, and if I had to select one piece of the puzzle for everyone with this issue to address immediately, this would be it.

Once the relief valve is open financially, continuing in medical practice becomes a choice, not an obligation, and the work simply feels more enjoyable.

We realize that not everyone can sell everything and move in with a friend, and many of us have children to support. From Shaun, "When I found myself in the midst of financial quicksand with no obvious vine to grab and the responsibility of supporting a family of five (and sometimes six), I took a different approach. Instead of slashing expenses, I focused on alternative sources of income including real estate, network marketing, speaking engagements, cosmetic injections, and administrative duties for our practice. As these ramped up, I've been able to decrease my dependence on clinical income to sustain my family. I am still a full-time clinician, but, I absolutely have options for reliable income should I chose to plot a different course." Again, once the relief valve is open financially, continuing in medical practice becomes a choice, not an obligation, and the work simply feels more enjoyable.

We know with certainty that every physician can decrease his or her expenses and expand other marketable skills. We have fallen into a one-track pattern, focusing exclusively on clinical medicine while buying houses, cars, fancy equipment, and high-end products, and spending unconsciously. This happens in part because we work extremely hard and we feel we deserve these luxuries. We have also fallen victim, yet again, to the "next logical step" syndrome and simply followed a traditional path of doing what doctors typically do, including accumulating debt, living in nice houses, and having nice things instead of renting one-bedroom apartments and buying dollar shampoo. We have also worn blinders to the idea that we can earn income outside of medicine, and we often neglect the other interests and skills that could both stimulate us creatively and sustain us financially.

The more you can reduce your expenses and generate alternate income, the more options you have, the more freedom you have, and, without financial pressure, the more joy you will find in medicine.

Look around your house tonight, and maybe you will see something you can sell, some cost you can eliminate, and more than one way to save. Rack your brain for ideas that you could pursue to generate alternate income. You can certainly use traditional thinking and continue to live with your current expenses, but if you do, make that a *choice*. Don't just stumble along on autopilot. If you choose to continue, then you are also choosing to continue being enslaved to your current salary's production requirements, leaving you also enslaved to the perils of modern medical practice. The more you can reduce your expenses and generate alternate income, the more options you have, the more freedom you have, and, without financial pressure, the more joy you will find in medicine.

What you can do to revive your situation:

1.   Track your spending honestly.

2.   Make a bare-bones budget, or at the very least, craft a non-negotiable savings and debt-reduction plan so you can eliminate your most burdensome financial constraints.

3.   Determine the lowest amount of income you would need to support yourself and your family in your current situation without any luxuries.

4.   Consider downsizing to a smaller home or a less-expensive vehicle.

5.   Consider selling barely used luxury items and parting with unused memberships.

6.   Meet regularly with a trusted financial advisor.

7.   Replace a mindset of "I deserve all these luxuries because I'm a doctor and I worked so hard to achieve this lifestyle" with "I deserve financial freedom." When making purchases, ask yourself, "Would I rather have this item I'm considering buying or freedom from financial bondage?"

8.   Earn extra income (locum tenens work, network marketing, speaking, medical writing, and the like) and put it directly toward debt or savings.

9.   If your student debt is excessive, take a position that offers student loan repayment in addition to salaried income. These may not be located in your ideal state or town, but working two or three years in a suboptimal area to eliminate your debt and gain financial freedom may be a viable solution.

10. Maximize your annual retirement-fund contributions.

11. If you are still in residency, plan to maintain your lifestyle at $55,000 annual income for another three to five years while you pay off student loans and create savings. Increase your lifestyle only when you have the money saved to do so. The Census Bureau estimated the 2015 median annual household income in the United States to be around $54,000; therefore, if you use this strategy, your economic position is still greater than that of half the US population.

12. Cultivate other marketable skills and interests so you are not dependent on income from clinical medicine to sustain you indefinitely.

13. Speak openly with your colleagues about money, and implement the strategies that others have used to free themselves financially.

14. Let others benefit from your example of streamlined finances. When others see the freedom of a less-expensive lifestyle modeled through you, they will be emboldened to make changes in their own lives.

What organizations can do to support providers:

1.   Host regular financial experts and seminars that truly benefit providers and are not simply selling investment products.

2.   Offer an employer match to 401(k) contributions, or offer other employer contributions to retirement savings.

3.   Have a transparent and clear compensation system.

4.   Offer multiple options for compensation that providers can choose from, such as one salary-based model and one production-based model.

5.   Allow providers to earn extra income through outside ventures such as locum tenens assignments, moonlighting, and consulting. Eliminate contract clauses that mandate pre-approval for outside income.

6.   Offer unbiased financial counseling to help providers get a handle on debt and to create reasonable savings and retirement plans.

7.   Allow and encourage providers to create flexible patient-care schedules that meet their needs. For example, offer work RVU or patient-care-hour targets based on employment status, but leave it up to providers to determine how those targets will be met.

8.   Offer compensation for work done in addition to clinical care—for example, hourly pay or work RVU credit for attending meetings, participating on committees, or performing community education or administrative duties.

9. Offer a CME budget that is separate from licensure and professional membership money—for example, $4000/year for CME, in addition to fees required for licensure, professional memberships, and maintenance of certification.

11.

DISILLUSIONMENT

*I can only find three kinds of business in the universe: mine, yours and God's.
Much of our stress comes from mentally living out of our business.*

—Byron Katie

It's perfectly acceptable to practice medicine simply as a way to earn money.

There, we said it. Generally speaking, millions of people go to work every day in fields that may or may not interest them, solely for the purpose of earning an income that supports their lives. Many of us medical types, however, entered healthcare as a calling or feel compelled to derive inherent personal fulfillment from our careers, with the money being important, but secondary. With this attitude, we find ourselves burdened by disappointment when our day-to-day responsibilities generate frustration instead of satisfaction. We look back at our mentors from years past and see that they seemingly had it all, and we wonder where we went wrong.

We have all likely known doctors now in their sixties or older who nostalgically report that they had glorious careers and wonderful patients and they feel absolutely fulfilled by their chosen profession. In fact, one told Shaun he has "never had a bad day in his life!" While this may be a bit distorted as our colleague reviews his career safely from the seat of retirement, the sentiment is clear: The medicine of yesteryear inherently provided intellectual stimulation, personal gratification, and enough positives that providers routinely worked well into their later years with no disillusionment or consideration of changing careers. They derived great satisfaction from their role as doctors, and the concept of burnout wasn't even on their radar.

We struggle to reconcile our original call to serve and our desire for career fulfillment with the realities of our daily practice.

As we have all experienced, modern medicine is a different animal. Although there are certainly days or occasions when we feel valued, appreciated, and genuinely happy to be physicians, there are far more days when we wonder, "What the *#@% am I doing here? Am I crazy? How has it come to this? Is this it?" To make matters worse, when we truly look into our hearts, we see resentment festering there. We resent our employers for making impossible demands, documentation requirements for stealing our time, our families for not understanding what we actually do, our patients for ignoring our well-intended advice, and, most of all, ourselves for getting us into this mess we call medicine. We struggle to reconcile our original call to serve and our desire for career fulfillment with the realities of our daily practice. This inevitably leads us to a fork in the road.

We ask ourselves, "Can I continue to practice medicine as a means to earn income with my existing skill set, without the fulfillment I imagined, or is the component of fulfillment so inseparable from my identity as a physician that I must change careers?" Our answers will vary individually, but in conversations with providers, we have learned that the disillusionment of working as a nurse or doctor without the fulfillment that they originally envisioned weighs heavily on providers' hearts. Working without fulfillment is so inconceivable to many providers that we feel absolutely imprisoned. We can imagine only three alternatives: joyfully continuing in medicine if the fulfillment is restored, miserably continuing if it isn't restored, or changing careers altogether.

Although this mindset is entirely relatable, we propose a fourth alternative: *What if we completely drop the expectation that medical practice is supposed to inherently satisfy us* and view it instead as a profession that earns income? What if we declare that we will compassionately offer our skills and advice to the best of our abilities to the clients we find in front of us at any given moment and then call it a day? What if we fully embrace that more than half of what we are required to do each day involves documentation and minutiae and the whole kit and caboodle simply earns us a paycheck? What if we then took that paycheck and spent it on experiences that built enjoyable relationships and fulfilled our hearts' desires? Could it really be that simple? Actually, yes.

From Shaun, "At times, I have gone so far as to call my hours spent in medical practice "fundraising," and I use the money earned on the job to fund family adventures and projects I find personally gratifying such as Save the Mothers and building my wellness team. I still provide the same compassionate patient care I always have at the office, and even though it's just the simple use of a word, it has made all the difference in my outlook when I head out in the mornings. I tell the kids half-jokingly, 'See you later, I'm off to fundraise!' and that feels so much different than leaving my family to begrudgingly trudge off to work."

We find that we're more dedicated to patients when at work than we used to be, knowing that medicine is only one component of a full and balanced life.

If you're worried that viewing your career as only a way to earn money will cloud your ability to care compassionately for patients, we encourage you to reconsider. In fact, we have noticed the opposite. In not requiring medicine to provide us personal fulfillment, we not only more readily enjoy our time in the hospital but can also appreciate the efficiency with which a career in medicine allows us to earn income that we can use to also enjoy the rest of our lives. Overall, with this attitude adjustment, our ability to wholeheartedly care for the patients in front of us has improved. We find that we're more dedicated to patients when at work than we used to be, knowing that medi

of a full and balanced life.

In essence, we have decided to view our medi

funds our lives instead of the be-all and end-a

doing so, *we have liberated ourselves from the need fo*

work to be any certain way. In changing our persp

trapped. We are consultants to our office patients, of   ..cm our best

advice, take it or leave it. We are data-entry clerks for our hospitals so

they can be successful businesses. We cover call to handle medical emer-

gencies and so our partners can get a break. We operate when surgery is

indicated and check our egos at the door. It's simple, really: We show up,

see the patients, do the operations, cover the call, answer the pager, type

in the EMR, go home, deposit our paychecks, and live our lives. When

patient interactions do bring us a moment of joy or satisfaction, they

become the icing on the cake and we can enjoy them for what they truly

are instead of clinging to them in desperation.

When we stop resisting the idea that medical practice can, in fact, simply be a

way to earn a living without requiring it to fulfill our souls, suddenly, the expe-

rience becomes much less stressful. So much of burnout comes from wish-

ing our profession was different and comparing what we imagined we

would experience to what is actually happening. When we embrace the

reality of our experience and use the income from it to fund relation-

ships and projects that truly fulfill us, we reclaim our sanity and our

enthusiasm for life. Our time spent on the job feels easier, too, because

we have stopped trying to find gratification in busywork, regulations,

and client demands, where it simply doesn't exist. Once we see that the

emperor truly has no clothes, it changes everything.

do to revive your situation:

1. Ask yourself if you feel resentment. If so, toward whom or what?

2. Brainstorm what you originally expected from your medical career in terms of personal fulfillment. Did you envision it as simply a means to earn income and a strategy for job security, or did you attach a different level of significance to this line of work?

3. List some important life events, such as weddings or funerals that you have missed because you put medicine first in your life.

4. Vow going forward to put your career in the back seat and to let your family, health, and enjoyment ride shotgun.

5. List specific accommodations or changes you will have to make in your workplace to realistically implement #4 above.

12.

DEATH BY 1,000 PAPER CUTS

*Being listened to and heard is one of the greatest desires of the human heart.
And those who learn to listen are the most loved and respected.*

—Richard Carlson

O ne year, Shaun and I made a list of all the things that had made us crazy over the prior two decades about medical practice. As you might imagine, the document contained obvious stressors, such as fear of lawsuits, train-wreck home-birth transfer patients, and being on night call, but the bulk of it seemed relatively insignificant. Our list included the following:

- Hospital accreditation suddenly requiring non-sterile speculums to be in individual plastic bags, making them nearly impossible to access with one hand during an exam

- Perpetual recertification requirements

- Written prescriptions required for breast pumps and over-the-counter medications

- Not wanting to call certain individuals or staff because of their sour and abrasive temperaments

- TV advertisements soliciting lawsuits for routine intrauterine contraception and for mid-urethral slings.

- Nursing calls requesting orders for over-the-counter medications or heating pads

- Our passwords expiring—constantly.

- Calls from case management about designating a patient as "inpatient, outpatient, observation, or outpatient in a bed" when we have no idea how to decide the correct designation for billing

- Pop-ups in the electronic record with every login

- The ultrasound machine deciding on its own whether to save pictures or not, based on what demographic data was entered

- Types of gloves, laparoscopy trocars, and drapes changing for each surgery depending on the facility vendor of the month rather than on surgeon preference

- Pre-authorization requirements for prescriptions that patients have been stable on for years

- Patient-satisfaction scores that drop when we don't prescribe the requested medication or see the patients emergently for non-acute conditions

- Patient information lost in electronic cyberspace

Our comprehensive list was much longer, but you get the idea. We each have our own list of kryptonite, things that are required for practice but that we feel absolutely powerless against within our given field. Some of the issues have plagued providers for decades, including patient non-compliance and disgruntled colleagues, but others, such as excessive clicks in the EMR and arbitrary compliance mandates, are newer and seem to be expanding exponentially. It's not that we're so fragile that we lose our cookies when we have to take a speculum out of a bag, change a password, close a pop-up, or write a breast-pump prescription but rather that these multiple tiny inconveniences (paper cuts, as Shaun likes to call them) add up incrementally, and soon, we are bleeding to death. Meaningless tasks, small annoyances, and arbitrary requirements keep getting added to our professional responsibilities, but none ever seem to be taken away. The tediousness and hassle become cumulative, and soon, physician burnout is inevitable.

The primary risk with this paper-cut problem is that as we expend most of our energy handling noncritical minutiae, when a true clinical problem arises, we are already severely depleted. Having expended all our reserves applying Band-Aids to tediousness, we end up calling on our leftovers, not our best selves, to actually provide patient care.

The primary risk with this paper-cut problem is that as we expend most of our energy handling noncritical minutiae, when a true clinical problem arises, we are already severely depleted. Having expended all our reserves applying Band-Aids to tediousness, we end up calling on our leftovers, not our best selves, to actually provide patient care. Naturally, in doing so, we make more mistakes, have short tempers, and have lower patient *and* provider satisfaction.

The employee disengagement so often discussed in administrative circles is almost never a disconnect arising directly from patients or clinical medicine but rather from a desire of physicians to distance ourselves from the paper cuts that constantly plague us. Restoring satisfaction to physicians, alleviating burnout, and thereby reviving our professional joy requires tackling these small annoyances with sincerity such that we, as providers, can focus our best energies on medicine, surgery, and compassionate care.

What you can do to revive your situation:

1. Make a list of your paper cuts.

2. Examine the list closely and pick one thing to try to eliminate, delegate, or at least come to terms with as a requirement. As we have discussed before, much of our distress is self-inflicted (as when we think, *I have to do this myself; no one else is capable of handling it for me*) or is caused by our resistance to a given requirement ("I shouldn't have to do this"), not caused by the requirement itself. For example, Shaun and I had to get over our resistance to speculums being in plastic bags and our resistance to recertification being required for our malpractice insurance. When we stopped wasting energy resisting the reality of these facts, our experience at work became more peaceful.

3. Try The Work, of Byron Katie, which can be found in her books or online, to help wrap your mind around the sometimes nonsensical reality of our profession—or any other areas of life you are struggling with.

4. Figure out exactly what you would need to make your experience at work more enjoyable, and ask your office manager or your administration specifically for those things (or create them yourself). For example, instead of complaining that your call room is inadequate, detail exactly what you need, and petition a manager. For example, the call room at one facility I worked for had no phone, no computer, a nonfunctional television, and the bedsheets were perpetually washed in a type of soap I was allergic to, giving me an unsightly rash whenever I stayed there. I complained behind the scenes for more than a year before making specific requests that were subsequently addressed.

5. If you have interpersonal conflict with a certain person, try these suggestions:

   a. Ask yourself what you don't know about the person's situation. Maybe they have a serious illness, their marriage is falling apart, or their home is being foreclosed. Personal problems are not an excuse for bad behavior, but realizing that everyone is struggling in some way may improve your compassion.

   b. Look for the things this person does well, and point them out directly and publicly. Even if all you can see is that he or she got dressed on a given day, say how great they look! Challenge yourself to find something to complement or appreciate about the person who annoys you most every week or every time you interact with them. Make it a game for yourself if you have to.

   c. Don't fly off the handle if a toxic person berates you or behaves inappropriately. Calmly state that you would like to have a discussion about the patient or situation when you are both less emotionally charged.

   d. Watch yourself closely. Maybe you are the one triggering the other person to behave aggressively or defensively. Can you change your approach such that the other person is not triggered?

   e. Request to meet with a mediator if interacting with a certain person is truly destroying your experience at work.

   f. Don't expect the other person to change in any way; instead, do what you can to defuse your interactions with them to be less stressful.

   g. Dedicate yourself to modeling professionalism in the workplace regardless of the circumstances.

What organizations can do to support providers:

1. Make absolutely sure that the compliance measures you are tracking are actually relevant to patient care. For example, several years ago, a well-intentioned "meaningful use" committee decided that physicians needed to target greater than 90 percent compliance in "printing the patient plan." This was tracked through the number of charts that had a box clicked and sent the document titled "patient care plan" to the printer. Sadly, no one tracked whether any information was typed into the patient plan or whether the plan was actually given to the patient. *Checking the box to print was the compliance measure,* so for every patient, we dutifully clicked the box to print the plan so our tracking was up to snuff. This yielded exactly zero benefit to patient care, as written instructions were rarely actually given to the patient. At the end of the year, the data presented showed that we had met our percentage compliance, and we were congratulated for improving patient care, though all we had really succeeded in doing was killing trees and wasting time.

2. Hire physicians with the intention of using them to actually care for patients, not to do tedious tasks. Realize that your best barrier to preventing patient-care errors, unsatisfied patients, and burned-out physicians is to give doctors the opportunity to dedicate themselves to clinical decision making, developing excellent bedside manner, communicating effectively with patients, and performing quality procedures. When a doctor has spent most of his day clicking boxes, filling out forms, and dealing with tediousness, he has no reserve to do the difficult task of patient care. Of course, then he is short-tempered with staff, unhappy, rushed through appointments, and not diligent in avoiding mistakes.

3. Hire adequate support staff to handle administrative and data-entry tasks so the physician can focus on patient care.

4. Train case managers, coders, and billers to figure out the correct insurance designation for patient stays in the hospital, and ask them to update the charts accordingly without asking the physician. We are not trained in these designations, and we have no working knowledge of how to choose the appropriate type of stay. Alternatively, if this is not possible, and federal or state law mandates that physicians choose the designation, convey this information clearly to providers and take the time to educate them accordingly.

5. Take care not to change gloves or procedure equipment without consulting the people who use these. Mistakes are more easily made when different equipment is introduced or tactile feedback is different.

6. Consider having mediators, coaches, or counselors available to improve interpersonal relationships and resolve conflicts between providers and staff who work closely together. Over the years, both Shaun and I have personally delayed or avoided calling certain individuals even when clinically indicated because we knew they would yell and berate us for disturbing them. Mediation is imperative when interpersonal conflict exists within the same office or workspace. Even when everything else is aligned, having to interact with or avoid a certain person because of that person's toxic demeanor can be disheartening to a provider.

13.

OUR LANGUAGE

If you want to change your life, begin by changing your words.
Start speaking the words of your dreams, of who you want to become,
not the words of fear and failure.

—Robert Kiyosaki

One year in college, my roommate and I attempted to give up complaining for the season of Lent. This concept intrigued me, as I had not previously viewed complaining as a luxury to be voluntarily surrendered. Throughout the experiment, my friend and I learned how integral complaining had become to our lives and how naturally it flowed in our conversations. It seemed like every few minutes, we had to correct our negative language, and the project never got easier. At first, without complaining, we had little to discuss. That season of Lent, we noticed that much of our relationship hinged on lamenting over anything and everything. In fact, we came to realize that we often watched our circumstances critically throughout the day to have something worthy of critiquing later. Unfortunately, decades later, my behavior hasn't much changed. I'm embarrassed to report I still spend much conversation time detailing every pitfall and nuisance of my professional life while simultaneously downplaying all the excellent parts.

In speaking with physicians in crisis, Shaun and I noticed a similar trend. *Those who are "burned out" speak constantly of problems*, impositions, mandates, administrators, government, documentation, and "paper cuts" while ignoring that, for example, they operated successfully on a patient last week, removing her tumor and saving her life. The happier docs clearly speak otherwise, reporting that they "crushed it" in surgery, even when the case was delayed for inexplicable reasons, and describing the baby they delivered at four AM as "so cute, and the mother pushed amazingly well!"

The truth is, we deliberately choose to tell the story of how awful it was to be on call last Saturday, how ridiculous the latest meeting was, or how the computerization of medicine is ruining our lives. We could just as easily tell the story of how special it was to welcome new life into the world during Saturday call, how intellectually challenged we feel to create collaborative solutions with our administrators, or how document templates have streamlined our notes.

Fortunately, consistent redirection of our storytelling to what went well instead of what irritates us can change our internal perception of our careers and ourselves. The truth is, we deliberately choose to tell the story of how awful it was to be on call last Saturday, how ridiculous the latest meeting was, or how the computerization of medicine is ruining our lives. We could just as easily tell the story of how special it was to welcome new life into the world during Saturday call, how intellectually challenged we feel to create collaborative solutions with our administrators, or how document templates have streamlined our notes. Even simply paying attention to how often we commiserate with each other over the plight of modern medicine can be revelatory.

Ask yourself, truthfully, when was the last time you discussed with a colleague all that was going well in your life? When did you last come home from work and relay the positive details of your day? If you're thinking there aren't any and this Pollyanna attitude is ridiculous, you're not only correct but also directly in touch with the larger issue at hand. When you look at your life and career, if you can't see any positive attributes or wins, a feeling of burnout is inevitable. Who could possibly feel valued, happy, or successful with an outlook of hopelessness and despair? Fortunately, relief is as close as your next conversation. *You have the option with every sentence of every day to share what went well or to focus on crap.* The way that you feel depends on it.

Working twenty-four or forty-eight hours on call with a new mindset is our best real-life example. From Shaun, "I decided to stop thinking of call as a demanding, inhumane experience and instead focused on the benefits that my shift yields my colleagues. When I'm on call, I feel great, no matter what is happening, because I know that my closest friends from the office are enjoying time off. I feel happy to take care of whatever arises, because I know my work is appreciated by my colleagues who are not working in the hospital during that time. In essence, I've decided I'm now taking call as a *gift* to my partners, not as a miserable obligation of my job, and that makes it far more acceptable than I perceived it to be in the past."

Ultimately, there are fresh ways to view every aspect of our profession, and to save ourselves from burnout, we can start with our language. By changing our minds and words to reflect even the smallest things that go right, we can relieve some of our burdens immediately.

What you can do to revive your situation:

1.   Notice what you discuss with your colleagues. Does it have a positive or negative tone?

2.   Notice how you feel when your colleague tells you a story about how awful a certain situation was. Realize that when you complain about everything, the people in your environment commiserate with you.

3.   Decide to be a leader, a trailblazer, a Pollyanna of professional and positive speech. Use your creative and intelligent brain to search for and speak about the tiniest glimmer of positivity you can find at your job. Reframe your mindset about your toughest dilemmas. Ask yourself how you can love documentation, what's great about maintenance of certification requirements, what's outstanding about being on call, how you can enjoy spending time doing data entry instead of clinical practice, and what's fantastic about your employer asking you to see more patients when you're already busy. It's an outrageous concept, we know, but you're up for the challenge!

What organizations can do to support providers and improve engagement:

1. How organizations speak to providers is critical, too. Pay attention to how you present ideas. I once attended a forty-five-minute administrative presentation with several colleagues about a new strategic plan. There were PowerPoint slides, diagrams, and spreadsheets, and it was all showcased with tremendous enthusiasm; however, at the end of forty-five minutes, my colleagues and I had no idea what the strategic plan actually included or how it was relevant to us as clinicians.

2. How administrators speak to providers can make or break engagement by displaying administrators' awareness—or lack of awareness—about our contributions. For example, a physician friend once told me a story of arriving for a seven AM meeting after working for the prior twenty-four consecutive hours. He had decided to attend the meeting instead of going home for a short break prior to his clinic day, which was scheduled to start at nine AM, meaning no sleep, no breakfast, and no shower. The meeting began with a high-level administrator complaining about the early start time and how he'd had to arise unacceptably early that morning to accommodate physician demands for meeting times. This type of language shows a clear lack of understanding and appreciation of physician contribution and should be avoided.

14.

DIFFERING AGENDAS

Peace cannot be kept by force; it can only be achieved by understanding.

—Albert Einstein

"When will you be able to see more patients? How can we get you to see more patients? Why aren't you seeing more patients? Can you see just two more patients a day?"

We've all been there, feeling deflated with yet another administrator posing yet another permutation of this question to our already beleaguered ranks. In my childhood, I remember my father, then the CEO of a small community hospital, speaking with exasperation at the dinner table about his physicians who "just didn't want to work." Now, decades later, Shaun and I have met hundreds of physicians who are experiencing the same exasperation when asked to increase their client load. Why do the powers that be keep asking this seemingly ridiculous question, and why are we perpetually resistant?

Perhaps the issue stems from simply having divergent agendas. It's no secret that hospitals are businesses and that businesses exist to make money in exchange for services rendered. Even nonprofit organizations care deeply about being financially solvent. And hospital boards naturally want positive recognition for their organizations through patient-satisfaction survey results, independent assessments, Internet reviews, media, accrediting bodies, and the like. As long as hospitals are earning profits and accolades, it appears that business leaders are doing their jobs.

doctors don't traditionally care much for five-star ratings or hospital profit but instead strive for peace of mind, for financial security, for intellectual stimulation, and to feel we have made a positive impact through the care we provide.

Alternatively, doctors don't traditionally care much for five-star ratings or hospital profit but instead strive for peace of mind, for financial security, for intellectual stimulation, and to feel we have made a positive impact through the care we provide. We have all stayed up late, worked on holidays, or gone the extra mile in some capacity to be sure our patients received excellent care. Who hasn't spent a vacation worrying about whether Mrs. Smith started insulin, if Mr. Jones is recovering well from surgery, or if Ms. Harris made it out of the hospital?

It's the interface between the two agendas that leads to some degree of distress and presents a great opportunity for mutual understanding. Hospital leadership likely went into business careers with interests and skill sets far different from those of doctors. They skillfully crunch numbers, make marketing plans, develop strategies for business expansion, generate revenue, and please boards of directors. Doctors help individual patients feel better as best we can with the tools available, and we treat the patient in front of us without much consideration for cost or reward. Because each patient has different needs and problems, each one is taxing in his or her own way. Fifteen minutes to discuss recurrent miscarriage, evaluate pain, or discuss a new diagnosis of diabetes is already grossly insufficient. When the administrative meeting asking us to increase production follows a long day of being rushed through appointments, it's easy to see why meltdowns ensue.

The solution is to find a mere sliver of common ground between clinical and administrative agendas. Those of us who are employed need to more openly embrace that we are, in fact, employed. This means we have agreed on some level to support the goals and objectives of our organizational leadership, which likely includes increasing annual profits. Unfortunately, when most of us agreed to employment, we noticed only the perks, such as paid malpractice, a stable salary, and benefits, forgetting to consider that as employees, we see patients to fulfill the vision and meet the financial targets set by our leadership, not simply for the sake of providing care. Likewise, hospital administrators must remember that most physicians were drawn into our profession for reasons that did not include generating business revenue or earning a five-star company rating.

The solution is to find a mere sliver of common ground between clinical and administrative agendas.

The feeling of burnout shows up most strongly when these financial discussions lack transparency. Have you wanted to pull your hair out following meetings in which you were asked to see more patients in the name of "excellent patient care," "patient safety," or "community access" instead of the actual reason, which was to generate revenue or earn accolades for your company? Having attended these meetings for years, Shaun and I have often wondered why the truth was never on the table. *Why isn't anyone saying, "One of our most important company goals is to be financially profitable, and our means to this end is through patient care. Let's have a discussion about how we can all collaborate on this goal while honoring our personal and professional ethics"?* It's as if no one wants to admit that, whether we like it or not, many of us are entrenched in the *business* of medicine.

To improve collaboration and engagement, we must begin with honest discussions. Administrators can be far more transparent about what they are asking us to do and why, and we can be far more accommodating in realizing that we are company employees. Similarly, administrators must absolutely acknowledge that seeing patients is not the same as producing widgets and that there is a level of human interaction that cannot be additionally compressed. Each provider has a maximum physical, emotional, and intellectual capacity that, when overrun, leads directly to burnout. Although standardization and perpetual increase may work reasonably well for assembly line setups, they have no meaningful role in patient care.

What you can do to revive your situation:

1. Evaluate who you work for. If you are employed by a hospital or an organization, realize that on some level, you have agreed to receive income in return for your contribution toward the *company's* goals (not your personal goals). The company's goals and your personal goals may or may not be congruent.

2. Understand clearly what the goals of your employer actually are, and ask yourself if you can reasonably contribute. If not, can you find any common ground?

3. Share your true needs with your employer and/or your partners. Use specific examples of real patient-care issues that require your time and attention and have you feeling pressured to provide less-than-optimal care. Present solutions, not just complaints, at these meetings.

4. If there is a complete mismatch between your values and those of your employer, you may be faced with a choice between continuing to work with this awareness or searching for a work environment that better matches your ideals.

5. *Stay focused on solutions.* Administrators trying to convince doctors to see more patients, and doctors trying to convince administrators it's not possible, all in the same meeting, year after year, is fruitless. Come to these meetings with fresh ideas. For example, propose what support you would actually need in order to effectively and safely see more patients (e.g., a scribe, more rooms, a different nurse or medical assistant). Volunteer to participate in pilot projects or to work with consultants designed to increase physician productivity.

6. Know and understand your personal limits. Work with your employer toward common goals, but do not overextend yourself at the expense of your mental or physical well-being, or to the demise of your treasured relationships. Productivity and personal well-being need not be mutually exclusive, though it is nearly impossible to negotiate reasonable productivity parameters when you don't know or respect your personal limits.

7. Don't expect your employer to inherently know or respect your personal limits. Only you know what you can safely and reasonably do, and you must stand up for yourself in these types of negotiations.

8. Approach your administrators and managers as collaborative partners. Maybe even make the outrageous move of asking them exactly what they need from you to be successful in their jobs as senior leaders. So often we focus on complaining and making demands, forgetting that we are only one part of a comprehensive corporate team designed to improve the health of our communities.

9. When and if your organization hosts a forum or requests provider opinions on a given topic, show up and participate wholeheartedly. We cannot expect our organizations to collaborate with us if we are not active participants in the process.

What organizations can do to support providers and improve engagement:

1. Be transparent and communicate your agenda clearly. It's not wrong to be a company that wants to increase profits, but it *is* wrong to go about it by trying to manipulate doctors into creating said profits in the name of patient safety or quality care.

2. Be clear during hiring about what's expected from providers. Let us know up front if we will be expected to increase patient volumes, and over what timeframe. For example, if you expect your providers to work at a level equivalent to 50 or 75 percent of MGMA production averages, delineate that clearly during the hiring process. Also clarify exactly what those expectations mean in terms of hours spent in the office, work RVU production, and number of patients seen per day.

3. Establish true common goals with providers, then work toward those goals collaboratively.

4. Recognize that each provider's physical and emotional ability to see patients may differ and that this capacity may vary with time. Have a baseline requirement, yet be flexible in annual productivity targets instead of requiring perpetual increase.

5. Be absolutely honest and transparent. Hostility arises when what is said does not match what is done.

6. Understand what physicians actually do, and demonstrate this understanding even in seemingly inconsequential areas such as scheduling meetings. For example, we know of providers who have been asked to attend meetings about improving patient access to appointments—*in the middle of their patient-care times.* Attending a meeting or training midday on short

notice means canceling or rescheduling patients. It's confusing to be asked to cancel patient appointments to attend a meeting on the problem of patients not having access to appointments.

15.

SELF-INFLICTED SUFFERING

Dost thou love life? Then do not squander time, for that's the stuff life is made of.

—Benjamin Franklin

Work is not empirically the most important thing in life, truly. If you are among the few who genuinely feel that it is, then you are likely not feeling burned out and are probably wondering why you're reading this book. Unfortunately, what has happened is that in dedicating ourselves to patient care, many of us have allowed our medical careers to slowly take over our lives, such that they have become the cornerstones of our existence. Have you said to your child, "Sorry, I won't be at your soccer game this weekend because I have to work," or to your spouse, "Sorry, I won't be home for dinner because I have to see a patient in the Emergency Department," or to your extended family, "Sorry, I'll miss the Christmas gathering again this year because I'm on call"? What about the things we say to ourselves: "I can't exercise this morning because I have to go in early and finish my paperwork"; "I'll make my husband's favorite dinner another time, when I'm not post-call"; or "I know I said I would be home on time tonight, but I promised Mrs. Jones I would be there for her labor and childbirth even if I was not on call"? We know these excuses too well.

> **What has happened is that in dedicating ourselves to patient care, many of us have allowed our medical careers to slowly take over our lives, such that they have become the cornerstones of our existence.**

We have insidiously decided that being available to our patients is more important than taking care of our personal health, raising our children, spending time with our spouses, and generally enjoying life.

Those of us at our wits' end are now feeling the repercussions of allowing our careers to consume our lives. The situation may have crept up on us from a genuine desire to serve, but there's something we have forgotten to acknowledge: The responsibilities we have assumed are entirely self-inflicted. We have insidiously decided that being available to our patients is more important than taking care of our personal health, raising our children, spending time with our spouses, and generally enjoying life. Some of us have fallen into a pattern of overworking ourselves to hide our social ineptitude or the fact that we feel irrelevant outside of the hospital. We bend over backward to see one more patient or to get up at night to deliver a baby, yet we can't be troubled to listen attentively to our spouses, make holiday gatherings a priority, or even reliably show up for dinner. We theoretically want to be home for family meals and feel distressed that nannies are raising our children, but we continue to choose work over family, over well-being, and over pretty much everything else.

In fact, when we take a deeper look, we realize not only medicine consumes us. When my marriage was suffering most, I pinned it on work responsibilities yet neglected to acknowledge that I was also electively taking an online class, training for a marathon, and fostering special-needs dogs. The issue was not empirically my choice of employment but my false declaration that the obvious demands of a medical career were ruining my life and relationship. The truth was that yes, my career was demanding, but I enrolled myself in the class, signed up for the marathon, and took on the care of homeless pets additionally and preferentially over valuing my spouse. Feeling overextended and stressed, I lamented only the "unreasonable" components of medicine and blindly ignored my role in overextending myself, disconnecting emotionally, and creating the problems that plagued me.

Similarly, Shaun says, "For years, I blamed my chronic exhaustion and lack of sleep on the overnight call schedule. It wasn't until one of our tea times that I truly saw the problem: I didn't go to bed on time, *ever*. It was just easier to blame the obvious negative thing than examine the root cause of always being overtired. I realized that even if I completely stopped being on call, the problem wouldn't resolve until I addressed the real issues. Accurate solutions lie in accurate assessment and, once examined, the situation could be changed. I changed the habit of staying up too late to going to bed at a reasonable time and my fatigue was drastically reduced, despite keeping the same overnight call schedule."

There will *never* be a time when our desire to help others or to overachieve dissipates, and there will certainly never be a time when our employers or patients ask us to be less available, to open fewer appointments, or to work shorter hours.

Here's our suggestion: Starting immediately, reclaim your life. Figure out what's important, and build your schedule around that. There will *never* be a time when our desire to help others or to overachieve dissipates, and there will certainly never be a time when our employers or patients ask us to be less available, to open fewer appointments, or to work shorter hours. In our profession, everyone always wants more, and our praise- or guilt-driven, people-pleasing, caregiving nature has gotten us into hot water. Of course there are increasing paperwork, documentation, and regulatory demands, as we have already belabored, but the situation you find yourself in is more likely self-created than externally imposed.

Likewise, there will never be a time when we start feeling less guilty; many of us feel driven to do more, and we struggle to reconcile what we are actually able to accomplish with how we expect ourselves to perform. Shaun and I have yet to meet providers who feel they are the parents, spouses, athletes, friends, or doctors they could or should be. As one of our colleagues articulated, "We all feel as if we're failing at everything just a little." It's a constant struggle to do everything well. When we're being the doctors we want to be, we feel guilty for not being home. When we're with family, we feel as if we have abandoned our patients. If we continue in medicine, the other aspects of our lives and health may suffer. If we quit medicine, our finances may suffer and we feel guilty for quitting or for disappointing those who trained us. There is no easy way out of this guilt predicament, and yet we have unintentionally painted ourselves into this corner.

We got here innocently, because we *care*—about our patients, our families, and our communities.

Many of us find ourselves working at night because we chose to be on call; we have overflowing schedules because we agreed to add on a few extra acutely ill patients; and we fear lawsuits because patients are litigious in the face of bad outcomes, yet we knowingly chose professions in healthcare. We missed breakfast because we scheduled surgery (or went jogging) at seven AM, and we missed dinner because we stayed late to document. In our remaining free time, we have likely committed to coach Little League, sing in the Christmas choir, and volunteer at the animal shelter, none of which we end up doing to the level we feel we are capable of. All of it feels like we're just scraping by, not delivering our best. We got here innocently, because we *care*—about our patients, our families, and our communities. We didn't purposefully overextend or exhaust ourselves. Doctors, friends, it is up to us to flag down the lifeboat and reclaim our lives.

Of course, it's much easier to pin our misery on the computer or other arbitrary demands on our time than to acknowledge that we've been careless with our most valuable resource and allowed the all-consuming heart of a caregiver and practice of medicine to take over. It's also easier to hide in the busyness of medical practice so we don't have to deal with our marriages, social lives, health, and the rest of our lives. These perspectives, however, are not only false but disempowering and leave no room for improvement.

The idea is not to overachieve or to do everything perfectly but to create a state of personal well-being in which you can consistently act and speak with kindness, professionalism, and compassion.

Don't worry. Take heart! You don't have to abandon your desire to help others, your natural empathy, or your caregiver's heart to proceed. Instead of constantly striving to achieve, to help more people, or to be the perfect spouse, parent, community leader, or physician, you can embrace the currency of kindness. This means no matter what you're doing, do it kindly. If you find that you're so overextended that you are not being kind in your interactions with others *or with yourself*, use that as the barometer for change. The idea is not to overachieve or to do everything perfectly but to create a state of personal well-being in which you can consistently act and speak with kindness, professionalism, and compassion.

What you can do to revive your situation:

1. Take absolute responsibility for your situation and your feelings of burnout. The degree to which you feel you have created your misery is the degree to which you will be able to create your happiness instead.

2. Identify your most basic needs and parameters. They can be as general or as specific as you prefer. For example, my basic parameters are restful sleep most nights, outdoor exercise four days a week, and enough emotional margin that I'm not short-tempered or checked out and am therefore able to engage in meaningful relationships. Shaun's are being engaged with family, feeling well-rested, and being able to take care of herself without feeling overwhelmed: "Once I find myself reacting in an irritated or short-tempered fashion, I reevaluate and realign."

3. Unapologetically reschedule or eliminate the self-imposed obligations that interfere with these parameters. Are you on a committee that meets at eight PM because it's more important than eating dinner with your family or because the achiever-career monster guilted you into participating?

4. Look honestly and ruthlessly at all the components of your career and your life that you have let creep in uninvited and make incremental adjustments until you feel well. Care for patients and participate in projects that are meaningful to you and that don't simultaneously ruin your life or steal your ability to be kind to yourself and others. Decide that you can continue on in patient care, have meaningful relationships, *and* be simultaneously dedicated to self-care. Identify healthy limits that are relevant to your personal situation and brainstorm creative solutions.

5. Use the same tenacity that got you through medical school and residency to create a work-life balance that is manageable.

6. Use the barometer of kindness to assess yourself. If you are not able to be kind most of the time or are quick to fly off the handle, chances are, you're overextended and running on empty. Take time to nourish yourself or to make changes accordingly.

16.

ELECTRONIC MEDICAL RECORD
AND DOCUMENTATION

*Trade you expectations for appreciation and your whole world
changes in an instant.*

—Tony Robbins

B ecause we have made these points ad nauseum elsewhere, let us
not waste another line of text here belaboring the perils of the
EMR and how it has seemingly transformed brilliant and creative clinicians into data-entry clerks. But let's also not understate the negative
effect this beast has had on many of our colleagues, forcing some into
early retirement and creating depression in others. (Shaun's darkest
times were actually inspired solely by ever-changing EMRs.)

So, let's cut right to the chase, to solutions and strategies that we have
used to reframe our thinking and to view the computer as an ally, not a
foe, in our practice.

Remember the days of the rotary phone, TV without remotes, and no
Internet? If you do, you are likely fortyish or older and have experienced
myriad technologic advances in your lifetime. This means that although
you may not know every nuance of modern electronics, you are certainly
an expert at learning how to use new technology. In the past thirty years,
you may have independently learned how to use a remote control, Atari,
VCR, DVD player, telephone answering machine, video camera, Walk-
man, DVR, Wii, desktop computer, laptop computer, Blackberry, iPad,
iPod, iPhone, Wi-Fi, cell phone, car phone, PlayStation, Internet, PowerPoint, e-mail, Skype, TurboTax, and any number of other programs.
You may also have taught yourself, without formal instruction, to be

proficient in the use of photo-optimization programs or video editing. How many hours of initial frustration did you experience with each of these? Surely some of you remember the agony of sitting down to watch your favorite TV program on VCR, only to find it hadn't recorded, or the distress of having to entirely retype a document you thought you had saved on a floppy disk. Shaun and I certainly do.

Were you excited to figure out new technology, or did you deem it a total hassle? Did you expect to struggle initially, knowing that you would become an expert with time, or did you give up after a few learning attempts?

The point of this trip down memory lane is to remind you that although many of us still can't figure out the TV remote (honestly, I'm afraid of the one in my home), we are all experts in learning how to use new technology. We've been doing it all of our lives. Shaun and I concede that EMR is not nearly as intuitive as iPhone, is more cumbersome than PowerPoint, and is not as much fun as virtual gaming; however, it's ultimately just another electronic to learn. It has bugs and glitches, we agree, *and we didn't ask to be forced into using it*, but we've got this; we're experts at navigating this curve. When Shaun and I decided to view our new EMR as just another technical device that we needed to learn, our resistance to using it decreased and it became a tool, not a detriment to our practice.

Oh, by the way, did we mention we're all doctors? All of us attended medical school and learned how to read EKGs, place central lines, interpret lab results, and assimilate volumes of information into our brains. Some of us even learned surgery. We are literally experts at learning; it's how we got to be where we are. So why do we work diligently and deliberately to learn the nuances of laparoscopy, robotics, or ventilators yet balk at the idea of using an electronic record? Is it really that much of a hassle?

After years of resistance, Shaun and I deliberately decided it wasn't. Once on board, we committed to becoming EMR experts in the same way we approached all other aspects of our professional lives. We aspired to know every trick, every shortcut, every possible way this beast could help us at work. We took optimization classes, solicited our more proficient colleagues to teach us, and spent hours creating templates to avoid typing redundancy. When we stopped resisting and complaining and instead approached the system with the intention of mastery, we saw progress, felt ease, and noticed a sense of optimism appear.

Shaun says, "I actually appreciate our new EMR and can find what I need quite quickly. The redundant portions of my operative and clinic notes are templated as are many of my discharge summaries and responses for normal results. I have patient instructions built into the home-going fields and laboratory data populates with the push of a button. My inherent thoroughness has not slowed me down and my charting efficiency is better than ever. Of course I still have my moments but overall merely changing my view of the EMR from an insurmountable obstacle to a tool I could master freed me from electronic bondage."

---

for many, the issue is not the computer, exactly, but the required changes in documentation that came with the computerization of medicine.

Now, we realize that for many, the issue is not the computer, exactly, but the required changes in documentation that came with the computerization of medicine. Physician documentation used to be for the sole purpose of recording a patient's concerns, relevant history, and physical exam, and delineating a treatment plan. If a lengthy explanation was required, it was to remind ourselves as clinicians what we were thinking or to clarify our logic for other treating providers. Today, the history, exam, diagnosis, and treatment are the easiest parts! The majority of the documentation involves selecting codes for insurance companies, writing the note in such a way that it meets certain billing criteria, and clicking through endless required pop-ups before the chart can be officially submitted. And, we write knowing that lawyers, auditors, and even patients themselves are reading the text.

There's also a solid muscle-memory component in gaining the speed to know where to look and click next in order to complete the chart. Long gone are the days of the simple note to convey medical information; instead, we are immersed in the drudgery of what often feels like nonsensical clicks. On this topic, we hear you, and we have little to add. Developing efficiency and eliminating as much redundancy as possible through document templates and streamlining order sets is truly the best advice we can offer to you.

To summarize our suggestions: First remember that you're an expert at learning and, more specifically, you're an expert at learning new technology. Think how far we've come from the library card catalogue, Atari, and recording songs off the radio onto cassettes! Next, stop swimming upstream; drop your resistance to the documentation required by EMR even though it's cumbersome and not something you voluntarily signed up to do. Decide that the EMR is a required tool of the trade, just like image-enhancement technology for photographers, and get after it. Lastly, decide to master your EMR, whatever version you have, and recruit the resources you need to achieve this. To master this tool, use the same diligence you used to learn a difficult or challenging component of medicine. Once you're a wizard, model your efficiency and help get your colleagues up to speed.

What you can do to revive your situation:

1.   Tomorrow, go to the most efficient *physician* EMR user in your office or hospital and ask that person to sit down with you and show you his or her tricks. I had our resident EMR wizard optimize my screen setup, and it improved my workflow overnight. The next day, she and I went desk to desk and showed the others in our group the same trick. Learning how to streamline your workflow elbow to elbow from a doctor who literally does the same job as you is much more effective than taking a random class or learning from someone in the informatics department.

2.   Ask your nurse or medical assistant to sit elbow to elbow with the most efficient clinical-staff EMR user in your office to learn their workflow. Try to use existing ancillary staff as much as possible for data entry so that when the chart gets to you, you can simply enter your note.

3.   Delegate all but the entry of your visit note to ancillary staff. Update the acute-problem list after the appointment, but train your nurse or medical assistant to enter history, medications, orders, allergies, and the like. I often hear this can't be done, even from physicians in my own practice, but I assure you that *your expectation*, not your staff, is the problem. In my office, I work with a different nurse most days, including individuals from the nursing float pool who know little about women's health. It's striking that at times, a nurse who works with me can competently order medications and update the history simply because I expect her to do this, whereas when she works with a different physician, that doctor is hunched over a computer late at night, updating the chart, under the assumption that the nurse can't do it correctly. Check yourself

on this: Are you making false assumptions or unnecessarily micromanaging? Do you trust your staff to enter data correctly?

4. Hire enough staff, and train them for this type of data entry such that you are not wasting time transcribing longstanding medical, surgical, or family history into the chart.

What organizations can do to support providers and improve engagement:

1. Develop the mindset that the physician's role in documentation is only to enter the clinical visit note in a way that justifies the diagnosis and medical decision making such that optimal care is provided.

2. Likewise, develop the mindset that it is the role of clerical staff, coders, billers, nurses, technicians, and/or medical assistants to handle the rest of the chart and get it up to snuff for the nonclinical aspects of care. Hire and train adequate staff accordingly.

3. Encourage physicians to learn optimal documentation from other proficient physicians in their field instead of from random computer training sessions. I once attended a mandatory class designed to optimize my use of the electronic record, and despite the fact that I am in the field of obstetrics and gynecology, the patient the trainers assigned me in the learning environment was an elderly male, with no option of switching to a female or pregnant patient.

4. Proactively arrange individualized training sessions for providers to help them create personalized order sets, note templates, common medication prescriptions, and the like to streamline their documentation process.

5. Willingly pay providers for the time they spend outside of the clinical practice of medicine and attending optimization classes and building the shortcuts that allow them to document efficiently. Remember that one of the primary reasons physicians are reluctant to see more patients is because each

hour of patient care means two hours of desk work. The more efficient that desk work becomes, the more willing providers will be to book additional patient visits.

6. Seriously consider hiring scribes for providers who request them. This strategy not only reduces physician busy work but also shows that your organization respects providers and intends for them to work at their highest level of medical decision making and patient interaction, not as data-entry clerks.

7. Offer physicians the option of high-quality voice-recognition charting, as dictating into the document is often faster and more comprehensive than typing.

8. Make sure your providers understand the resources available to them within your organization. For years I read a monthly newsletter suggesting the medical informatics department could help me with computer issues if needed; however, I never called because I interpreted this to mean computer hardware problems. I later learned from a friend working in informatics that most of the department was there to help nurses and doctors troubleshoot issues with patient care programs and clinical documentation, and, that these people were available to help me real-time even overnight. Thereafter, I actually called the department and realized how helpful it truly was.

17.

KNOWING WHEN TO TAKE TIME OFF

My religion is very simple. My religion is kindness.

—The Dalai Lama

The first patient of the day tearfully left my exam room, and I rushed around in the hallway. Of course I genuinely empathized with her condition, but I couldn't ignore the fact that on some level, I felt anger as well. I felt angry with the system, the scheduling desk, and even, inexplicably, with the patient for having a problem that had required a lengthy discussion beyond the allotted ten minutes. Embarrassingly, I almost felt worse about starting forty-five minutes behind schedule and disrupting all my downline appointments than I did about the suffering of my first patient.

As I fretted about the disrupted schedule, I suddenly caught myself. Who was this woman feeling annoyed with a patient in distress and feeling anger instead of compassion? The physician I knew myself to be had historically bent over backward to ensure that patients felt cared for, willingly saw overflow appointments on her days off, and sent personalized handwritten follow-up notes. In that moment of anger, I absolutely didn't recognize myself. Clearly, an intervention was needed. Where had my heart gone? What had happened to me? Who was this cruel imposter wearing my skin?

It was following this one patient interaction that I decided to put myself in time-out. I didn't know exactly what that would look like or how I would manage financially, but I knew something serious had to be done. I had no intention of practicing medicine with anger for patients or normalizing such distorted emotion. My state of mind was unacceptable, and I became acutely aware that any hardship required to make a course correction would absolutely be warranted, even if it meant starting from scratch. I felt convicted that living in a tent out of the back of my car would be better than advertising myself as a caregiver and then subsequently showing up without heart. Armed with the recognition that I did not at all want to be an uncaring physician or a seemingly heartless human, I negotiated a six-month unpaid sabbatical and examined my choices.

During my time off, I felt my compassion return, appropriate emotion revive, and enthusiasm for both my career and my life bubble up to the surface. With rest, introspection, time away from constant demands, and the luxury of unscheduled time, the version of me who had felt called to practice medicine in the first place reappeared. *Leaving medicine completely felt wrong, yet going back to the rat race seemed impossible, too.* Part of me wanted to run for the hills, while the rest of me felt like a total failure, a weakling, and a sore disappointment to those who had invested so much in my training.

Ultimately, I returned with a more flexible schedule, less pay, and more margin to regroup incrementally if I felt myself slipping. These changes worked wonders, and now, in the same hospital, with the same staff and the same administrative and work environment, I feel hopeful, valued, and compassionate in my care. *The system didn't change; I did.* Although I still feel the constant pull to work more hours, add more patients, and overextend myself, I now know the ugly consequence of this practice, and I refuse to go back.

Shaun took a different approach. She explains, "I identified my values, rearranged my schedule, and continued to work full time while dedicating myself to personal development outside the office. It has been through this practice of taking responsibility for my emotions and my life, and dedicating my mind to finding creative solutions, that I have transformed my experience of medicine. Instead of taking a sabbatical, I moved incrementally while working full time over a number of years to reach the level of satisfaction I currently enjoy." Again, *the system didn't change; she did.*

Both pathways are viable alternatives for reviving the joy in medicine, or for discovering that a different career suits you better. In utter frustration and looking to end our careers, both Shaun and I discovered that leaving abruptly wasn't truly aligned with our values, and *we figured out how to work comfortably in the system and community we serve*. For others, this may not be appropriate.

Look in the mirror. Do you recognize yourself? Are you treating yourself and interacting with others in productive and meaningful ways, or are you going numbly through the motions, getting angry, and hanging on by the skin of your teeth? If you are in survival mode or, worse yet, disengaged from patients as I was, clearly it's time for a change. For some, a day off, a massage, and a minor attitude adjustment will be adequate; for others, this won't be enough. You know what's best for yourself, and you know whether your behavior is harmful or unprofessional. If you're not sure how you're acting, ask your staff or a trusted colleague to give you an honest opinion. Often, it's easier for those we work closest with to see that we've gotten off track than it is for us.

There is no reason to wait for a crisis, meltdown, health scare, or broken relationship to begin traveling a more peaceful path.

Be bold, be honest, be courageous, and do whatever needs to be done to revive yourself and your life. Better yet, if you feel only slightly annoyed and a twinge of apathy or fatigue, begin the process of inquiry and self-care immediately, before you spiral the proverbial drain. There is no reason to wait for a crisis, meltdown, health scare, or broken relationship to begin traveling a more peaceful path. As many a guru has said, no matter how clearly our problems seem to be externally derived, the real issues and their solutions are within us.

What you can do to revive your situation:

1. Take an honest look at your office behavior. Are you being kind? Are you interacting with others appropriately? Are you easily triggered? Is your attitude toward patients compassionate or incredulous? Do you describe every patient as crazy? Are you feeling panicked in the hospital parking lot on your way in to work? Are you afraid of your pager?

2. Take an honest look at your personal behavior. Are you drinking alcohol every night to forget the day? Are you taking sleeping pills to quiet your mind? Are you happy or annoyed to see your family at night? Do you feel as if everything and everyone wants something from you?

3. If you don't like the answers to the above questions, decide to live differently.

4. Take small actions incrementally or take unscheduled time off as soon as it is feasible, to reevaluate your personal and professional choices. (My sabbatical officially began six months after I decided that I needed the time away, as it took that long to arrange alternate care for my patients.)

5. Don't resign yourself to feeling trapped by outside forces. Instead, use your creativity to make different choices going forward that allow you to respect yourself and enjoy your life.

6. Don't settle for a curmudgeonly, perpetually irritated, disappointed, unprofessional, or exhausted version of yourself. Set the bar higher. Lead by example to show others that there are pathways to peace of mind that do not include suicide or giving up medicine. Decide to lead the pack in taking responsibility for yourself and your happiness, and show others that trying something is better than resigning yourself to misery.

7. Talk with your employer or manager about options for sabbatical or vacation.

8. Actually take *all* your allotted vacation, and enjoy it without charting, reading work e-mail, or checking on patients remotely.

9. When you do take time off, don't schedule every minute of it full of projects or adventures. Give yourself the luxury of unscheduled time to truly decompress. Observe how easy or difficult this is for you.

10. Discuss with your employer or manager the specifics of what margin and/or support you need to enjoy your existing practice, or to improve your demeanor.

11. Complete the Maslach Burnout Inventory–Human Services Survey (MBI-HSS), a validated burnout self-assessment. You can find this online. The scoring gives the healthcare provider scores on the three traditional components of burnout: emotional exhaustion, depersonalization, and diminished sense of personal accomplishment. You can use your scores to assess your current situation and to track changes over time.

What organizations can do to support providers and improve engagement:

1. Encourage providers to actually take their allotted vacation each year. Help them find reasonable coverage of their clinical responsibilities while they're away so they can rest and not have to work remotely on pseudo-vacation.

2. Support a sabbatical policy that allows providers up to six months away without automatically losing their positions. (We are not suggesting this has to be paid leave.)

3. Encourage providers to participate in personal development and leadership programs that help them work and live at their highest levels. This approach is different and far more valuable than encouraging providers to simply maximize productivity.

4. Do not encourage any employees to work until they crack or become so burned out that they behave inappropriately. Having an organizational culture or agenda that values productivity over well-being is extremely dangerous and yet is pervasive in modern medicine. It is far more challenging to acutely rehabilitate a toxic physician than it is to support and encourage well-being incrementally. Be flexible and innovative about this.

It is far more challenging to acutely rehabilitate a toxic physician than it is to support and encourage well-being incrementally.

18.

WHAT TO DO NOW

Information without application leads to zero transformation.

—Jamie Beeson

For Physicians

Congratulations! If you've read this far, you are clearly dedicated to reviving yourself and your life by tackling burnout head on. We have presented multiple ways for you to take action, and we hope some of our suggestions have resonated with you. Even if they have, assimilating so many ideas can feel overwhelming and you may not know exactly what to do now. If you've marked a chapter or an idea that struck you, return to it and get started. If you're still feeling stuck or find yourself paralyzed by analysis, consider the following three-step approach.

1. Address your basic needs first, starting with rest. When we're exhausted, we can't think straight. Look at your schedule immediately and book a day or a week of unscheduled time dedicated to simple refueling. *This is different than booking time off to complete your extensive to-do list.*

2. Tackle crises next. Is your marriage on the brink of collapse? Are you about to get fired because your documentation is incomplete or your interactions with people are toxic? Are you addicted to drugs or alcohol? Is your health acutely at risk? Begin fixing whatever is most in danger.

3. Assess and modify your work and your life as you see fit. You can begin by asking yourself *Do I feel trapped, and if so, by what exactly? Is it my schedule, the expectations of others, my financial*

situation, guilt, obligation, my family, or the personal investment I have already committed to medicine? Is it something else entirely? Whatever the reason, write it down. Now ask yourself truthfully, *Am I truly, honestly, inextricably trapped, or is this situation something I could change if I absolutely needed to?*

Your answers will reveal the truth of your perceived imprisonment and offer clues to your ultimate liberation. If you discover you've taken a wrong turn somewhere, have no worries; relief is as close as your decision to continue or to make a course correction. The good news is that your past choices led you to this exact juncture and that the future is entirely in your hands.

For Organizations

Congratulations! If you've read this far, you clearly care about your providers and wish to run a humane, innovative, and efficient business. We have presented multiple ways for you to take action, and we hope some of our suggestions have resonated with you. Even if they do, however, assimilating so many ideas can feel overwhelming and you may not know exactly what to do now. If you've marked a chapter or idea that struck you, return to it and get started. Most importantly, take these or other ideas to your providers and ask for their input. Transparency, honesty, communication, and collaboration are the keys to your success in improving provider well-being and reducing burnout.

You could begin immediately by asking each of your providers what they need to improve the quality of their experience at work and then move forward by tangibly beginning to fulfill their requests. Additionally, you could host a grand rounds or workshop on the topic of physician burnout to open the discussion at your facility. Ultimately, remember that happy, engaged providers are integral to the success of your organization in terms of patient satisfaction, patient access, organizational accolades, revenue, patient safety, and quality of care. Genuinely and proactively partnering with providers can improve the integrity and solvency of your business. We commend you on taking this situation seriously.

AFTERWORD

As we are met with the challenges of modern medicine, we inevitably come face-to-face with the ultimate questions "Why am I here?" "What's my purpose?" and "Do I even matter?" To find answers, we can look to the circumstances of our lives and try to make sense of them. When we evaluate patients, employers, responsibilities, and paperwork, the answers seem hidden, and nothing makes sense. Initially, medicine seemed to provide a clear path to feeling useful, selfless, and relevant; in the thick of it, however, medical practice can feel more like a charade than compassionate service.

After having arrived with certainty of our significance to humanity, we find ourselves inherently questioning who we are and our contributions. We thought that becoming physicians would guarantee our societal relevance and prove our value to ourselves, yet now we realize, in the midst of disillusionment, that we were wrong.

The truth is, there is simply no inherent, long-lasting satisfaction in any career, relationship, or accomplishment; even less so if achieved under duress. And by now, you likely understand our belief that there is absolutely no guarantee our choices will create happiness in our lives. Ultimately, true happiness does not come from how or with whom we spend our time. To be at peace and feel an authentic sense of value, we must dedicate our lives to the single purpose of infusing the world with genuine kindness and love for others as well as ourselves, and we must do so with utmost integrity. Whether we are kind to our patients as doctors, to our children as parents, to our employees as CEOs, or in any other societal role is irrelevant if it's not coming from genuine kindness within ourselves. If we first care for and are gentle with ourselves, we can be authentic in sharing love and compassion, thereby feeling the sense of fulfillment we ultimately long for.

We know that as you read the chapters in this book and went through the exercises, you have realized that the joy we all seek does not automatically come from changing employers, rearranging our schedules, or cleaning up our finances. These tactics may be necessary to create space in our lives and to get us out of survival mode, but in and of themselves, these changes will not create joy.

The adjustments we have discussed in this book can create margins that we can then use to get back in touch with our hearts, our compassion, and our capacity for genuine love. From there, our paths in the world will become clearer and we will come to realize that our joy does not hinge on what we do or who we are but rather on the degree to which we put genuine kindness into the world. As long as we are thrashing around in sheer survival mode, this perspective is impossible; however, as we reevaluate our life choices, align with our values, and change our minds about our perceived roles, we recognize that it is not the details of our lives but our capacity to love that is a far greater service than any facet of medicine could ever be. It is our capacity to empathize with others and to live in the world as genuine healers that encompasses the entirety of our value, and therein resides our ultimate joy.

ABOUT THE AUTHORS

SHAUN J. GILLIS, MD	MELISSA WOLF, MD
Raised in a small town	Raised in a big city
Married	Not married
Has children	Has no children
Travels with checked luggage	Travels with a backpack
Flawless makeup	No makeup
Leans politically right	Leans politically left
Christian	Nondenominational
Prefers skiing and kickboxing	Prefers running and yoga
Extrovert	Introvert
Night owl	Morning person
Doer	Thinker
President of multiple organizations	Worker behind the scenes
Prefers long-term patient relationships	Prefers acute-care patients
Full-time physician	Part-time physician
Has had one job post-residency	Has had multiple jobs post-residency
Network marketer	Massage therapist

MELISSA WOLF, MD, FACOG, CHC, LMT

Melissa Wolf, MD, received an undergraduate degree from Cornell University in 1996 and a medical degree from State University of New York at Buffalo in 2000. She then completed five years of residency, including one year of Family Medicine training and four years of training in obstetrics and gynecology. Following residency, she worked as an obstetrics and gynecology physician in rural Tooele, Utah, for three years as part of the National Health Service Corps Scholarship Program. In 2008, Dr. Wolf joined Bozeman Health Women's Specialists, where she specializes in general women's health, pregnancy care, and female surgical procedures, including vaginal hysterectomy. She completed additional postgraduate study in health coaching at the Institute for Integrative Nutrition and is a licensed massage therapist in Montana. Dr. Wolf has also worked extensively with underserved populations, spending several months of 2015 in a South Sudan women's hospital with Doctors Without Borders, and providing ongoing locum tenens medical coverage in critical access hospitals across Montana. Additionally, she published a humorous and informative women's health book in 2012: *Do You Have a Tipped Uterus? 69 Things Your Gynecologist Wishes You Knew.* Dr. Wolf has extensive professional speaking experience, has been featured on Discovery Health's *Babies: Special Delivery* and on Medscape. She is also a marathon runner and in 2013 completed the Ironman Coeur d'Alene triathlon.

SHAUN J. GILLIS, MD, MS, FACOG

Shaun J. Gillis, MD, received her undergraduate degree in microbiology in 1990 and her master of science degree in microbiology in 1993, both from Montana State University. She worked in molecular biology for two years, then attended the University of Washington School of Medicine, completing her medical degree in 1999. She completed residency training at the University of Rochester and began practicing general obstetrics and gynecology in Bozeman, Montana, in 2003. She has had a particular interest in improving the quality of life for women with pelvic prolapse and urinary incontinence and has thus done additional training in that regard.

Dr. Gillis has been active in organized medicine, including being a delegate from ACOG to the AMA, and serving on the board of trustees and executive committee of the Montana Medical Association (MMA). She served as MMA president 2012–2013. She remains active in the state obstetrics and gynecology association, currently serving as chair. She is also chair of Save the Mothers–USA, helping decrease maternal mortality in Uganda and eastern Africa.

Dr. Gillis has been married to her husband, Rick, for 26 years and has three children: Ian, Avery, and Eric. Their family opens their home to those in need, so there are often more than five people at the dinner table.

Her other interests include kickboxing, reading, hiking, and camping, in addition to being actively involved in her children's activities.

Dr. Gillis enjoys public speaking and, along with Dr. Wolf, has developed a workshop for helping physicians find their alignment.

PROFESSIONAL SPEAKING

Both Melissa Wolf and Shaun Gillis have extensive professional speaking and coaching experience. We are available for and enthusiastic about personalized coaching, professional speaking, and leading workshops on multiple topics, including physician burnout. For inquiries, contact us at TheOtherSideofBurnout@gmail.com

ACKNOWLEDGMENTS

This book has been several years in the making, through both our personal experiences and the process of translating those experiences into relatable concepts and workable solutions. Along the way, multiple people helped and encouraged us on the path of personal and professional development. We could not possibly name all of them here, as that alone would fill another book. Specifically, we wish to thank our instructors in medical school at SUNY Buffalo and University of Washington School of Medicine, our mentors in residency training at University Hospitals of Cleveland and the University of Rochester, our physician colleagues across the nation who boldly shared their personal stories and support with us, the many and varied organizations that have employed us, the patients who have taught us far more than we could have ever taught them, our coaches, our families, our partners, and each other for unwavering encouragement. Special thanks to our manuscript reviewers for their extremely valuable feedback including Heather Fork MD CPCC, Sara Bishop RN, Kirsten Drake PA, Linda Waring MD, Keith Waring PE, Kenneth May MD PhD, Elizabeth Luehder RN, and Corinne Moll MD, and to Dog Ear Publishing for creating our finished product. Lastly, we wish to thank those of you who have taken the time and initiative to read through this book and consider changing your mind or your circumstance for relief. We feel your struggle, we know your pain, and we admire your courage in moving forward.

CPSIA information can be obtained
at www.ICGtesting.com
Printed in the USA
BVHW062340100719

553087BV00013BA/376/P

9 781457 557002